The Future of IoT

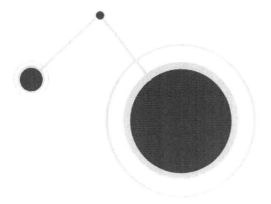

The **Future** of IoT

Leveraging the shift to a data centric world

Written by
Don DeLoach, Emil Berthelsen, and Wael Elrifai

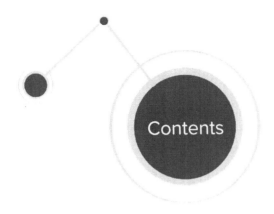

Contents

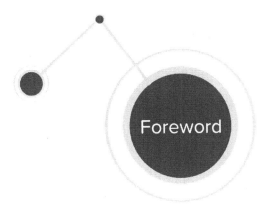

Foreword

Though I was flattered when Emil Berthelsen, IoT Analyst at Gartner Group, and Don DeLoach, co-chair of the Midwest IoT Council, asked me to provide the foreword and contribute to their book on the Internet of Things, I thought I'd better read it, just in case the ideas were too crazy … or not crazy enough.

Our world is full of machines and data, and with the IoT sphere continuing to cast a shadow over so many facets of our day-to-day life, data will increase exponentially from where we are today.

Like many of you, I've been in the big data, machine learning, and Internet of Things gig long enough to assemble an impressive collection of battle scars from use cases and technologies that were closer to bleeding edge than cutting edge. Don and Emil have similar bumps and scratches, in addition to ones earned in the trenches of the CRM and analytic database battles.

The theme is consistent; it's always about data, information, and knowledge. Connect the right data points and you can substantiate any result. The critical issue isn't whether any data *can* lead to a conclusion, but *why* we choose to ignore the rest of the data that's there, and there's always a surplus.

IoT, indeed technology, in general, has often had the goal of depersonalizing decision-making, even while making the outcomes more personal. The coming decade will be an opportunity to shape the innovations, freedoms, indeed, the lives of the planet's population for the next half-century.

As one would expect, this book talks about use cases, system architectures, and recent innovations. It also takes a confident stance on concerns around privacy, data ownership, and practical approaches to creating an IoT-enabled organization. What we do with IoT is still unknown, but there are a growing number of us in the industry, who hope to redouble our efforts to use these prizes—shared treasures mined of our universal human innovative spirit—towards better companies, communities, and shared prosperity.

Those of you who would think to pick up a book like this are the leaders, the tinkerers, the innovators, and the ones who don't follow a path but, instead, create a new one. Don and Emil are cut from the same type of cloth. They are inventive thought leaders, who have composed a powerful IoT guide for those who are getting started. This book will help you get started thinking about the IoT, all that data, and how best to use it. In this, a dissertation on data primacy, the First Receiver, and the progression of the IoT market, they've sensibly blended just enough crazy to get readers to think about IoT—and how data is the key element in driving the value to make the aspirations of IoT the reality of tomorrow.

~ Wael Elrifai

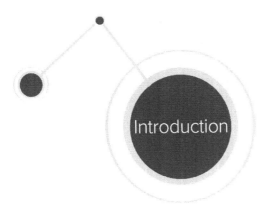

Introduction

From Smart Connected Products to System of Systems, Shifting Focus to the Enterprise

At this point, much has been written about the Internet of Things. Many who weren't paying attention before have become enthralled, while others may be growing tired of hearing yet another "oh so smart product" story. Smart cars, smart grids, smart homes, smart watches, and more are filling our airwaves, our stores, and our lives. So why another book on IoT? For the same reason people still write books about IT architectures, or real estate, or raising kids. We evolve. And while considerations about real estate and raising kids may change slowly over time, the path forward tends to be more aggressive when technology is involved. Erik Brynjolfsson and Andrew McAfee's recent book *The Second Machine Age*, did a wonderful job in highlighting how the basic advances in physics associated with technology and the combinatorial element of new technological ideas create an almost hyper-acceleration of technological advance. So the world in 1980 may have looked entirely different than the world in 1960, the world in the nineties was much more different still than the eighties, and by 2000 it was changed on an even more radical scale. And yet, the progress since 2000 is a quantum leap from all of history up until then, and in five years, will be another quantum leap forward still.

There have been certain critical steps along the way. The semiconductor and the microchip, to be certain, were two of them. The computer and then the personal computer were two more. Cellular technology for certain. And then there was the Internet, which, in and of itself, was spawned from an initial military and academic effort (as many are) called ARPANET. But when Sir Tim Berners-Lee developed the "map," if you will, called the World Wide Web, and Marc Andreessen at the NCSA at University of Illinois developed Mosaic as a graphical, intuitive interface to the web, the Internet had its underpinnings to move from the realm of what was possible to what was practical, and they paved the way for the web becoming mainstream. Technology becoming mainstream defines the beginning of the wave.

To reduce this discussion to the limited examples here does not do justice to the evolution of technology, but it conveys the idea that certain seminal ideas take root in a way that effect our society at large. What's more, these waves actually occur in phases of maturity. The Internet, which started as not much more than an insecure vehicle for looking at marketing brochures, has evolved into an elaborate system where thousands, if not millions of applications are used by billions of people each day. Use cases ranging from ERP to sales force automation to banking to photo sharing, once restricted to either physical process or applications that would never be considered for external hosting or deployment over the Internet, are now the rule and not the exception, but this didn't happen overnight. It matured in phases.

Now we have the Internet of Things. In some ways, it too has a long history. The IoT, as we know it, began to see life around 2008 to 2009. Kevin Ashton from MIT is largely credited with coining the term and has been a key driver since then. By 2011 it picked up steam. Some called it "the Semantic Web" (namely, the W3C organization founded by none other than Sir Tim Berners-Lee himself), some called it "M2M (Machine to Machine) Communications," some called it the "Internet of Things." There were other names as well. And if you were looking, you would have seen more and more buzz about it in the market. There was the "Peggy Smedley Show" that interviewed person after person, company after company doing things in M2M, and increasingly IoT. There were books like Daniel Obodovski's *The Invisible Intelligence*. And there were companies beginning to place big bets that this would become the "new new thing."

One of the most prominent was IBM and their "Smarter Planet" initiative. From 2012 to 2014, we saw the likes of Cisco, GE, Siemens, Ericsson, PTC, and numerous others going all in on IoT. And while IBM was early to the game, Cisco, PTC, and GE were undoubtedly all in. Cisco framed this with their "Internet of Everything" (IoE) initiative, and authored an oft-quoted paper projecting 50 billion connected devices by 2020. GE went all in as well, ranging from their general advertising around the new connected world, to establishing a software excellence center in San Ramone, California, to the introduction of GE Predix, the "operating system for machines" to talk to each other, and the corresponding ad campaign centered on attracting new talent for the effort. Then there was PTC. The company that had evolved from its origins in computer-aided design (CAD) and Product Lifecycle Management (PLM) and acquisitions of Computervision, which had previously absorbed Prime Computer, its lineage was all about product design and development. If you were building products, PTC probably knew you, and you them. PTC, especially their CEO Jim Heppleman, seemed to embrace the Internet of Things and in 2013 purchased ThingWorx, an IoT development platform. Many would soon suggest they overpaid, but the fact remained they were seemingly committed to the space. They reinforced that with the acquisitions of Axeda (Machine Cloud), ColdLight (predictive analytics) and others, basically doubling down on their IoT focus.

In late 2014, Jim Heppleman, along with famous Harvard technology professor Dr. Michael Porter, co-authored what would become a seminal article about the Internet of Things in the *Harvard Business Review*. In it, they described what they saw as the likely evolution of the Internet of Things. The progression seemed to make sense to us, as it did to many. Simply stated, there were five specific stages of IoT's evolution. The first was the "product" stage. Simple enough. An air conditioner is an air conditioner. We get it. The second stage was the "smart product" stage. So now we have a programmable air conditioner. As technology evolved, it became possible to put computational power, even if it was minimal, into products like an air conditioner. In doing so, the air conditioner might be capable of adapting to certain conditions, or changing settings based on time of day. This was quite an advance.

Then came stage three, which is "smart connected products." Now the air conditioner is accessible by the Internet. This has big indications. You can control your air conditioner from your phone. The company providing the air conditioner can look at its operation at a component level, and compare that to millions of other units to do predictive maintenance, so when it "sees" certain markers in the data, it can dispatch a service agent. This is a critical stage. In many ways, this is where much of the market focus has been. This is where, in 2017, a great deal of the focus and understanding remains, but it won't be for long.

The subsequent two stages, as outlined by Heppleman and Porter, are more meaningful than most people seem to understand, but is indicative of the broader focus in the market. It is where the broader market will begin to shift focus from the product provider to the enterprise. The fourth stage is "product systems." This is where the smart thermostat talks to the connected HVAC and the smart window blinds and heated floors. In some ways, this is common sense. It's reasonable that all functionally related elements should be "connected" to "talk to each other," or more specifically, interoperate. One of the earliest indicators of the inevitability of this phase was Google Nest Division integrating Big Ass Fans, after which, the Nest Thermostat communicated with the smart connected Big Ass Fans. The battle over the smart home is one of the early proving grounds of this stage.

The practical (or impractical) reality of smart connected products in the home suggested there was a need for them to work together, so key industry players began to jockey for dominance. This pertained to the communications standards, as well as the ultimate command and control platforms ranging from Apple HomeKit to Amazon Echo to Google Home, Samsung SmartThings, and others. The Allseen Alliance (primarily driven by Qualcomm) got involved to broker standards for consumer IoT as well. And while the focus today in most elements of IoT is still largely on smart connected products, the progression to product systems is clearly happening.

Larger players, like GE and Hitachi, bringing forward solutions like GE/Predix and Hitachi Lumada, further demonstrate this. In some ways, these are the industrial/commercial equivalents to HomeKit or SmartThings. This might also suggest that if you have a factory or hospital or distribution center running Predix or Lumada, you might benefit from having, respectively, GE or Hitachi smart products connected into these platforms. And while these will allow other products to coexist, there is an implied level of tighter integration when you connect a specific company's products into its platform. This is not to suggest that Predix or Lumada are equivalent. There are many differences, but they both are designed to contemplate a larger ecosystem.

This isn't new. We have seen Apple leverage iTunes for years, where iPods, iPhones, and more all very seamlessly coexist. They will work with Windows, but is that really what you want? Apple makes billions of dollars by leveraging the accessibility of their products to meet a variety of their customer needs. They make it easy. That is a big play for GE, Hitachi, and others, but before we explore this further, let's look at the fifth and final stage.

"System of systems" is the fifth and final stage. Think of this as your home appliances talking with your home security talking with your home entertainment talking with your car and your wearable devices. The reasons for this will be beyond obvious soon enough, but consider what you can begin to do if the data—the information—from these devices can be shared. Imagine appliances working with energy systems in order to coordinate maximum efficiency. This includes recharging electric cars at night. The HVAC isn't only looking at temperature, but air quality, and based on input from your wearables, may adjust such things as temperature, humidity, and airflow to suit your preferences. The entertainment system may interact with the lighting system and security system to adapt to certain conditions, ranging from when you are way from home to when intruders are detected on your property.

Beyond somewhat obvious examples of basic system-to-system interaction, enriched signatures gain value when further enriched by either other non-IoT operational systems (like your personal schedule that informs the security system, the energy system, the entertainment system, and your cars, as to when they need to adapt and in what manner) and even by external data, IoT or otherwise, like weather data, traffic data, etc.

All of this information contributes to the generation of a richer signature, which can create greater insight and actionable intelligence to enhance productivity and quality of life, and, on a commercial level, can enhance competitiveness, profitability, and quality of work life. To say people and organizations should care about this is an understatement. Nobody would carry a flip phone, along with a separate text pager, camera, dictation device, mp3 player, video player, compass, and myriad of other devices; they carry a smart phone. You want to fully leverage the resources at your disposal in the most effective way. IoT will become the ultimate integration. To not leverage all the available data would be to artificially curtail the use of that data and restrict what would otherwise be incremental and meaningful insight.

Perhaps the most profound examples will be in the delivery of healthcare and the operation of smart cities. There will be people who live better and longer because of IoT, whether they realize it or not. Some people get excited about IoT because it's a strong business opportunity. Others see it changing the world.

Effectively leveraging data from IoT will deliver the greatest value, and here is where it gets really interesting. If the value created is a function of your ability to leverage the data—then who controls it? Who owns the data? Who can use the data? Why? How does this happen today, and why? And how will it happen in the future, and again, why?

Let's consider the Heppleman/Porter thesis on the progression of IoT. Product companies provide smart connected products. The majority of the effort to create and deliver IoT technology has been aimed at the product providers, so the myriad of IoT platforms out there are being sold to product providers as a platform for them to deliver smart connected products. This is where the market is. This is where the money is. So, this makes sense.

In most of these products, the sensor devices in the products are designed to talk to the "machine cloud" of the product provider, where the appropriate controls are executed and historical analysis in conducted, so the product company can provide predictive maintenance and better servicing. In other words, the sensor devices create sensor data, and that data is consumed by the application associated with the products operated by and owned by the product company. It is a closed-loop, message-response system. In many cases it is compelling, to be sure, but it is hardly open and leveraged beyond a minimal point. But again, the stage of smart connected products suggests the money to be made will be a function of meeting these, albeit basic, demands.

When we move to product systems, the interoperability and more importantly, the underlying association of the data from IoT system A to IoT system B may or may not be deliverable via one product company. It is certainly in their best interest to do this, because, in these circumstances, they make more money and retain more control. This is why large product companies are spending so much to provide interoperability between their related products. As the market continues to demand that products from different companies interoperate and share data, the

orchestration and delivery of data will likely become more difficult. When you contemplate "system of systems," the logical focus
goes from the product company to the enterprise or organization
that has invested in numerous IoT subsystems.

Shifting your focus from the product provider to the enterprise changes the game. An aha moment comes when you realize
an organization's ability to leverage underlying IoT data is a function of its ability to own and control that very data. When the
market makes its way from stage three to stage five, the focus will
most certainly shift from the product provider to the enterprise.

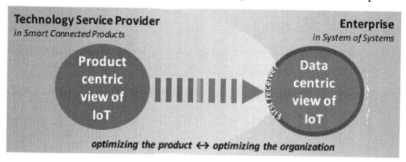

In doing so, the whole concept of ownership and control of
the data should be re-cast. This isn't to say the product provider
shouldn't see the same data they were getting before. They should.
It just means they shouldn't get that data at the expense of the
enterprise that owns and uses the IoT subsystems. And while
this may seem to be a big problem, in fact, it's technologically
quite simple. It has to do with architecture and governance. The
issues are commercial and economical. And with the right architecture and related accommodations, everyone can win. There
can be a fairly simple component in the equation called the "*first
receiver*" that can make the effective propagation and leverage of
IOT data a reality.

The *first receiver* would basically sit inside or behind one or
more edge devices at a given entity (factory, hospital, retail store,
etc.) and provide the ability to persist the data coming off a variety of IoT subsystems associated with that entity. The data would
be stored into a master data model for that specific entity which

could be then cleansed and enriched, and where the underlying data could then be propagated, either to local, consuming applications or constituents (like the point-of-sale or inventory system at a local store), and/or to remote constituents or applications as well. For example, the retail store may propagate one set of information to the regional headquarters, but a different set to the national headquarters.

The *first receiver* would likely also propagate (under contract) all the HVAC data to the HVAC vendor, just like it did before the *first receiver*, but only the HVAC data, nothing else, and likewise for the other product providers. In fact, it might also send a different subset of data to supply chain partners, and another set of data to OSHA, the FDA, or other regulatory monitoring bodies. The *first receiver* would also provide accommodation to the product providers to maintain their firmware, much like we see today with printer drivers. They would also likely enhance security as well. In short, the *first receiver* concept is designed to allow the maximum leverage of the utility value of IoT data. The *first receiver* ensures the right data gets to the right constituencies at the right time.

This won't come easy at first. Product providers have too much to gain by "owning" everything. They all want to be Apple, but in today's market, market drivers will dictate a more open, democratized set of capabilities. And this is the focus of our book. We believe the key value—the maximum value—will ultimately come from leveraging the utility value of IoT data. For this to happen, one needs to travel from the world of "smart connected products" to the world of "system of systems," and understand the basic underpinnings of what will deliver, or inhibit, that progression.

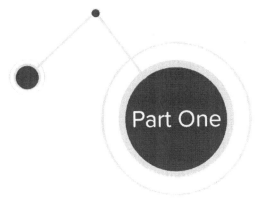

Part One

From M2M to Today: What Is "Here" and How Did We Get to This Point?

"If you look at history, innovation doesn't come just from giving people incentives; it comes from creating environments where their ideas can connect."

–Steven Johnson

Chapter 1

A Perfect Storm: Rapidly Changing Circumstances

Industry leaders are quickly recognizing fundamental changes in their industries and markets. The Internet of Things is changing a world of monitored and remotely managed devices and products to a new and innovative environment of opportunities for enterprises in smart machines, shared data, business models and services. This perfect storm of cheaper sensors, lower connectivity costs, higher bandwidth, improved data processing tools and capabilities and innovations in business processes and models all contribute to the shift from products to processes in IoT.

Early days of machine-to-machine (M2M)

Impressive progress in innovations and technology developments marks the last five decades. Technology achievements include transistors, microchips, personal computers, the Internet, satellites, mobile phones, and even unmanned aerial vehicles. Any enthusiast will quickly add and extend the list with protocols, sensors, compute power, cloud technologies and data analysis. Telemetry, telematics and SCADA (supervisory control and data acquisition) technologies accompany these developments, referring to machines sending signals or messages to other machines, which can interpret the messages and take actions such as issuing alerts or triggering mechanical responses.

Telemetry, telematics and SCADA have formed and led to M2M (machine-to-machine) of today.

Signaling or messaging between machines isn't new. RADAR, SONAR and RFID are examples of the use of broadcast radio or sound waves, delivering new insights to proximity awareness. What M2M and, more so, IoT adds or requires from networks is two-way communications between machines, enabling a substantially richer infrastructure of sensors and actuators.

In M2M, the focus is on devices, networks and applications. It is the combination of these three capabilities: devices capturing data, networks transmitting data, and applications converting data into actionable information that has delivered value to industries and enterprises. Particularly, the capability of managing real-time data has made the difference. Let us look at some examples:

- **Track and Trace:** With location sensors mounted in everything from all forms of transport (bikes, vehicles, boats, trains, and so on), to containers, to parcels, to elderly monitoring, child and pet tracking devices, and to hospital equipment, track and trace applications deliver the benefits of quickly identifying where items are located.

- **Smart Parking:** Sensors are used to monitor when parking spots are free, then that information gets posted into an application that people can access to understand availability. The message is the location of the available spot, and the response is the driver using this information to park faster and easier, saving time and fuel.

- **Smart Lighting:** This can mean a number of things, ranging from how you set up and control the lighting in your house, to the deployment of smart lighting in buildings, parking lots, and streets and public areas and use occupancy (motion) and luminescence sensors to determine when lighting is required and when it is not. The message is the notification of movement or notification of the absence of adequate light, and the response is to turn on (or off) the lights, saving energy.

- **Waste Management:** This refers to sensors in the city trash receptacles that detect when they are near full, informing city services when they need to be picked up (or not picked up, as the case may be). The message is the notification of the bin being full, and the response is the city services pick-up, saving resources and time. In enhanced models, environmental factors such as smell have been included in the pick-up request frequency.
- **Vending Machine Servicing:** Sensors are deployed to monitor the inventory and the temperature of the vending machines. The message is the inventory count or the temperature, and the response is the route service person making a trip only when necessary, and in doing so, having the right inventory or the right tools to address the needs of the machine, saving time and money.
- **Security Perimeter Control:** This can take a variety of forms, but at the most basic level, these are motion sensors detecting the presence of someone or something where they should not be. The message is the location of movement and the response is the deployment of security resources to ensure the safety and security of the location, saving time and money.
- **Temperature Monitoring:** This is basically a thermostat, monitoring the temperature of a given room (or so many variations) and taking action as a result of hitting certain thresholds. The message is the temperature, and the response is turning on or off the air conditioning or heat as defined by the configuration, saving energy and increasing comfort.

There are many more examples of M2M examples, ultimately aimed at delivering remotely monitored and managed solutions as illustrated in Figure 1.1: The Progression from M2M to IoT [Source: Machina Research, 2015].1 located on the next page.

The progression in M2M connections is one from connected devices to monitor and manage operational performance to managing and remotely controlling devices, again for improved operational performance but also beginning to deliver improved customer experience (as in the examples of waste management, smart parking and other applications).

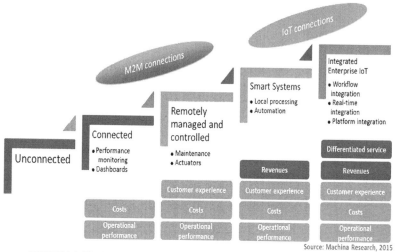

FIGURE 1.1: The Progression from M2M to IoT [Source: Machina Research, 2015]

M2M is primarily peer-to-peer communication. As M2M predates the wider adoption of the Internet, M2M relied on satellite, terrestrial phone lines, or cellular technology to transfer data, bringing with it the limitations of addressability and tended to exist in proprietary, closed-loop systems. Factory automation remains another example of M2M where machines would be networked with each other in the factory so they could "know the state" of the other machines on the factory line. These would operate on a token ring or Ethernet network without external interaction.

M2M was expensive, and remained initially within the realms of the military industry but as productivity improvements became more commonly associated with M2M, implementations began to emerge in discrete industry sectors. The perfect storm hadn't yet arrived.

Arrival and influence of the World Wide Web

ARPANET and the World Wide Web are recognized harbingers of the Internet but each has its own history and legacy, and to understand developments in IoT, understanding these roots are key.

Leveraging developments and theoretical insights in packet switching by JCR Licklider, Leonard Klienrock, and Laurence Roberts, all from MIT and working independently, ARPANET went live in 1969 as a system to share academic and military information, connecting a small number of computers at UCLA, Stanford, UC Santa Barbara, and the University of Utah. Over the next few years, they would add several other universities then begin to add sites like AMES Research Facility for NASA, Mitre, Burroughs, and RAND. What was key in the development of ARPANET were two technical developments in packet switching and the implementation of TCP/IP, both to be key features in the Internet. ARPANET was officially closed in 1990.

As one curtain closed, another opened, and the World Wide Web, as a shared information space where documents and resources are identified by Uniform Resource Locators (URLs) and connected by hypertexts was just about to emerge. The World Wide Web builds on many attributes of ARPANET, but significantly differs in critical areas such as access for everyone, not just scientists and academics. Originally set up on the NeXT machine in CERN, the World Wide Web was finally placed in the public domain in 1993, available with an open license to encourage dissemination.

The World Wide Web Foundation, also driven by Sir Tim Berners-Lee, outlines five core principles and ideas[1] of the World Wide Web, which to some degree have characterized IoT as well:

1. Decentralization (no central authority or controlling node)
2. Non-discrimination (net neutrality)

---

[1] Sourced from the World Wide Web Foundation, http://webfoundation.org/about/vision/history-of-the-web/.

3. Bottom-up design (code developed and shared with everyone)
4. Universality (interoperability of computers)
5. Consensus (developing universal standards through an open, participatory process in the W3C)

What we have seen in the Internet of Things are some of the same qualities of universality, bottom-up design, and decentralization. Consensus is still taking place with the formulation of standards across the many verticals and industries addressed by IoT. And while not on exactly the same overarching lines of any central authority or controlling mode, the IoT ultimately looks to establish autonomous entities and groupings, which reflect self-management and self-control.

It's interesting to draw the lines between the developments in M2M—from tightly controlled and centralized systems—and the developments in the Internet, which reflects degrees of openness, flexibility, and draws upon the five ideas and principles of the World Wide Web. These become even stronger messages when the Internet of Things becomes the next evolutionary step from the Internet.

The beginnings of the Internet of Things

There are many definitions and understandings of the Internet of Things. One definition refers to the "Internet of Things (IoT) (as) the network of physical objects or things, digitalizing information about the environment, and exchanging that data across the existing Internet structure." There is significant strength in this definition, but then narrowing down an emerging concept and market disruptor has its limitations.

IoT builds on expertise and experience from telemetry, telematics, SCADA, and machine-to-machine (M2M), and yet IoT differs from these architectures in fundamental and important ways as illustrated in Figure 1.2: The Changes in M2M to IoT.

In telemetry, telematics, SCADA, and M2M, the architecture adheres to fairly traditional IT approaches: fixed solution parameters with robust and solid design principles, focusing on the interworking of the application, the devices, and the connectivity component. All processing and data storage remained centralized.

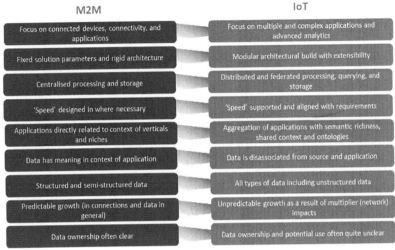

Source: Machina Research, 2016

FIGURE 1.2: The Changes in M2M to IoT

For the architects of IoT solutions, significantly greater flexibility and modularity is involved in the architecture, recognizing that changes may be made at any time, and that architectural builds may need to be extended with new requirements. In the IoT framework, abstraction between various functional layers of the platform stack becomes key, and interoperability between heterogeneous components paramount. In IoT, applications and the abstracted data become the real focus point, acknowledging that IoT architectures will continue to develop and expand, and that exhaust data, as generated by the sensors and processing, should be recognized as assets in themselves.

With data becoming a central asset in IoT solutions, the ability to handle all types of data, structured as well as unstructured and anything in between, becomes critical. Whereas data is given meaning in the context of the application in traditional M2M, in IoT, data is disassociated from source and application. Even the way in which data is processed, queried and stored in a distributed and federated way requires new approaches including edge analytics and fog computing.

So far, we have discussed some of the characteristics of IoT, but what has actually brought about the emergence of IoT for enterprises here and now? The Internet of Things becomes the culmination of many of the following developments in a perfect storm.

The perfect storm for the Internet of Things

Cheaper devices, including chips and modules, cheaper connectivity, cloud services delivering highly scalable and cost efficient as-a-service options, and improved data processing and management capabilities are what make this perfect storm.

Cheaper and smarter devices including chips and modules

Devices including chips and modules have started to become cheaper. The effect of economies of scale in IoT are beginning to impact production and manufacturing costs, and markets are experiencing significantly lower prices for connected devices.

One simple example of this trend is provided by an IoT solution provider in Canada, delivering artificial lift optimization technology. Any failure or disruption to oil production is an extremely expensive affair related to both the cost of the machinery and the lost revenue. Yet, with costs for a device being $15,000 to $30,000, the investment was hard to justify for an entire oil field. Ambyint, with its new device at a price of $1500, including the basic services of data capture and analysis, transforms the business model completely. There are similar price developments in such devices as imaging devices for vision analytics in production by FLIR Systems or communications modules in the emerging LPWA technology space by STMicroelectronics, Atmel, or Texas Instruments for Sigfox as example.

The additional development in devices is that for many of these components, either at the chip, module or device level, the device is actually becoming smarter. These traditionally had extremely limited processing and data storage capabilities as well as power. Today they are designed with enhanced levels of processing capabilities, storage and power, enhancing the potential functionality of IoT applications, and also enabling additional architectural concepts such as edge analytics, fog computing and ultimately, automation at the edge.

The combination of cheaper and smarter devices removes one of the fundamental cost barriers in IoT solutions, and adds to that perfect storm for IoT.

Cheaper connectivity

Short-range connectivity, such as Wi-Fi, ZigBee or other similar technologies, has always been available to M2M and IoT. This form of connectivity will remain the dominant form for around 70 percent of all IoT applications between 2016 and 2025.[2] A key reason for this development is the actual characteristics of IoT applications; the vast majority of connected devices being within buildings, homes or Wi-Fi enabled locations. There are, though, many other mobile or remotely located IoT applications in the connected car, connected industry, or connected energy, which require substantially wider coverage and real-time transmission of data. In these applications, the two main wireless technologies have been cellular networks and satellites.

For both cellular networks and satellites, data traffic has had the shared characteristic of being relatively expensive compared to other connectivity technologies. Satellite networks, especially, have been exceedingly expensive, potentially at $5 to $7 per MB. As the adoption of M2M and IoT has grown, and data traffic becomes more frequent, prices for cellular and satellite connectivity are coming down, and with the emergence of low-power, wide-area connectivity technology, designed specifically for M2M and IoT, the feasibility and affordability to use these forms of wide area wireless connectivity have been realized.

---

2 From Machina Research Global IoT Forecast Database.

Cloud services delivering highly scalable and cost efficient as-a-service options

With the growing number of connected devices generating continuous streams of data, another challenge has been that of data storage costs. What the market has experienced though is a dramatic fall in data storage pricing, from millions to thousands of dollars for 1 GB to one or two cents in the cloud. Once a major decision point for many enterprises, the accumulation and storage of data is no longer a financial concern for most industries. The shift from storage to processing and analyzing the data has become the focus in IoT.

On a side note, the added developments in cloud services, enabling immediately scalable resources for both processing and storage has further accelerated the focus on data as a new asset in enterprises. While many industries continue to "protect" their data by adopting on-premise or hybrid cloud solutions, more and more enterprises are implementing hybrid approaches dependent on the nature and importance of the data. This becomes a particularly interesting field to watch as we develop the concept of the *first receiver* approach in the book, and how cloud services and edge analytics delivers an important component to the architecture.

Improved data processing and management capabilities

These developments have little value unless all the data is properly stored, processed, and analyzed. Parallel to these developments in M2M and IoT architectures (developments in devices, connectivity, platforms, applications, and as-a-Service services), the management and processing of data was, in itself, undergoing a major transformation.

The challenge and problem of storing all this data, or what has become known as Big Data, hinges on the fast that scaling and managing centrally stored data was inefficient and remained expensive. Every new TB meant a hardware expansion. Not only were traditional data warehouses or datamarts expensive, the type and scope of data these databases could manage was also limited. Enterprises have been storing and managing data in relational database management systems (RDBMS) such as Oracle, SAP, and IBM. Enterprises discovered these RDBMS solutions had limitations and needed to be augmented and integrated with other solutions such as NoSQL and NewSQL,[3] allowing enterprises to work with different data types.

With these challenges, new innovations such as Hadoop with HDFS (Hadoop Distributed File System) and MapReduce appeared. What Hadoop and HDFS brought to the market was a new way of storing data in a distributed fashion, spread across several clusters, and managed as one central file system, providing a highly-scalable and reliable data storage solution. As the data was now distributed across several clusters, resilience was removed as an issue and storage could take place across a multiple of options including cloud. Overnight, Hadoop made it possible to manage and store all this data.

The second development mentioned was that of MapReduce. As data was distributed across several clusters, there was a potential for data queries to become exceptionally slow and cumbersome but through the approaches of MapReduce, the processing and analysis of data across distributed structures had little impact on speeds and capabilities.

With connected devices converting and sharing digital data in real-time, the market has seen two developments: that of Big Data and Fast Data. To address the latter development, data management and processing has experienced many new innovative technologies such as enhanced and improved data ingestion techniques, massive parallel processing, and, of course, in stream and real-time data processing.

What the perfect storm has enabled is the generation and transfer of data in quantities beyond imagination years ago and in real-time. This opens the opportunities for new IoT applications

---

3 For further reference, read Machina Research Note, "Why NoSQL databases are needed for the Internet of Things" (April 2014).

and services no longer focused on the actionable insights based on historical data, but on as near, real-time as possible data. This Fast Data attribute is what enables key concepts such as automation, self-driving, self-healing systems, as well as improves and enhances approaches and requirements in security, network balancing, scheduling, and new service development.

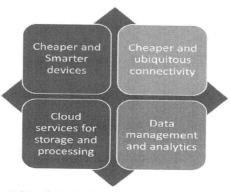

FIGURE 1.3: The Making of a Perfect Storm for IoT [Source: Machina Research, 2016]

Where is IoT headed?

The change from M2M to IoT is truly a shift from machine-to-machine communications to what today is referred to as IoT or Industrial IoT (IIoT). According to the Industrial Internet Consortium, the IIoT may be defined as "an Internet of things, machines, computers, and people enabling intelligent industrial operations and using advanced data analytics for transformational business outcomes. It embodies the convergence of the global industrial ecosystem, advanced computing and manufacturing, pervasive sensing, and ubiquitous network connectivity."[4]

What is important about the IoT is that it has moved from being an additional IT and/or OT enablement architecture and application in M2M to what is significantly more transformative for any industry and enterprise. IoT is a framework of change where data becomes king, and all enabling and supporting

4 Industrial Internet Consortium, "Industrial Internet Reference Architecture," version 1.7, p. 9.

infrastructures, architectures, and business process should aim to securely manage and exploit the data.

More and more innovative services and business models are emerging because of IoT. These include new commercial pricing models such as consumption-based, value-based, and outcomes-based pricing models,[5] where customers and clients pay according to either usage, perceived value, or agreed outcomes of IoT implementations. Examples of consumption-based pricing include user-based insurance by Progressive Insurance in the US or pay-per-horsepower for Rolls Royce airplane engines as part of their TotalCare package. For value-based pricing, companies such as Pirelli and Michelin can go one step further by embedding sensors in the tires of customer cars, and provide data about "the driver, his habits, his style of driving, the places where he/she more frequently goes etc."[6]

The consumption-based and value-based models may be suitably priced but they do leave to an element of risk with the customer/client. The outcome-bases pricing model is fundamentally a risk-reward model but significantly designed around the improvements and benefits from IoT that a customer/client achieves as "guaranteed" by the service provider. In this latest model in IoT, the expectations of improvements from IoT are so great that service providers such as Hitachi Insight Group are willing to undertake longer-term commercial arrangements on this basis.[7]

IoT will disrupt all industries and enterprises. It isn't a question of if but when, and enterprises need to be prepared for these

5 These three pricing models were recently announced and highlighted by the Hitachi Insight Group, as three models that enterprises would be presented to and relations established on.

6 Article by Giulio Coraggio, "IoT – Changing the future of the connected world!" http://www.gamingtechlaw.com/2016/05/iot-changing-future-connected-world.html.

7 See for example the twenty-seven-year agreement between Hitachi and UK Transportation Department, where Hitachi will manage the rolling stock and digital railway infrastructure in the UK, and sell this as a service based on outcomes

changes. With all this data in movement, one important area in the future will be data governance, and before we dive into the benefits of a *first receiver* approach, it's important to understand how the current closed-loop model started and how it works.

Chapter 2

Building Smarter Connected Products

Smarter, connected products enable a substantial range of benefits and opportunities in IoT. From providing monitoring, remote control and management capabilities to efficiency and productivity mechanisms and, ultimately, automation within any connected product value chain, few limits to innovation emerge. From the viewpoint of the enterprise, the importance of quickly realizing the benefits and opportunities in IoT is what drives the trials and business cases. It is worth exploring each capability and how increasingly value is returned to the business.

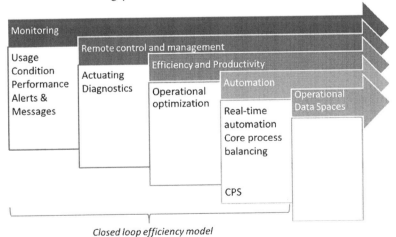

FIGURE 2.1: Capabilities emerging from smarter connected products
[Source: Machina Research, 2016]

Monitoring

The history of IoT can be traced back to early telemetry and telematics solutions, delivering the earliest examples of connected devices to monitor usage, condition, and performance, and through alerts and messages, improve the overall management of different operational processes. This could range from monitoring production lines, to drilling equipment at oil and gas sites, to being embedded in defense and space vehicles, and in monitoring the long stretches of pipelines, networks, and remote weather stations.

Basically, telemetry and telematics solutions have enhanced operational processes by enabling enterprises to monitor remote locations and equipment, reducing costs for 24/7 manning and/or receiving more timely information on process failures or poor performance. Being able to monitor processes in near real-time has also added to the overall operational performance of such machines as racing cars, aircraft, and ships.

One fundamental development that did need to take place to enable remote monitoring to work to its full extent was wireless communications. Without continued developments in quality and coverage of radio frequency, including satellite and cellular technologies, the value of remote monitoring would not have been as great as it was.

Remote control and management

A "next step" development, from being able to monitor connected devices, is to enable actuation that is remote control and its management. Achieving this sounds like a strange task until you begin to explore the requirements in terms of the connected device itself (and its configuration), the type of connectivity used, and ultimately, how to manage thousands and thousands of commands to different devices at the same time.

Within the configuration of remote control and management are the steps receive and analyze the data from the connected devices, defining immediate actions or commands, and looping these back to the devices, or other devices in the wider solution. This could, for example, be information from an agricultural solution, measuring the level of moisture in the soil, and potentially issuing a command to turn on a watering system for a given amount of time to reach a defined, set level, or perhaps a home automation system, which provides temperature readings from a home, and automatically initiates air conditioning systems and window blinds to reach a cooler temperature with less sun impacting the levels.

Remote control and management has also meant further developments in associated technologies. At the device level, actuation capabilities have become an important feature of M2M and IoT solutions. Previously, modules were mainly configured with a sensor, very limited processing capabilities, and a wireless connectivity solution and antenna, sending alerts and messages. With the requirements of remote control and management, particularly including actuation, connected devices now require additional processing and actuation features as well as two-way communications in connectivity technology.

Another feature of remote management, which has had significant implications for IoT connected devices and their associated lifecycles, are over-the-air updates. For many connected devices with lifecycles in the five- to twelve-year periods, and more importantly, installed in remote and potentially hard-to-access locations, remote management that includes feature updates has become a very important attribute in IoT. With two-way communications, connected devices have had to become significantly more flexible and open in their structures, enabling future configuration development and, as will be seen later in the book, opening the path towards fog computing and edge analytics for automation.

IoT has moved the goalposts from passive monitoring to a more direct interaction between the connected devices and the enabling IoT platforms.

Efficiency and productivity

Beyond monitoring, remote control, and management, the next development emerged from opportunities in working with data from connected devices in real-time. M2M applications were designed with narrow functionality objectives, and connected devices were part of the design architecture to capture and generate the required data from the environment for the specific applications. In IoT, following a growing amount of data generated and transmitted by connected devices in real-time, opportunities to analyze this data further and potentially for purposes other than the M2M application became a recognized opportunity. Data from connected devices was used for the designed M2M/IoT application but soon became an asset that could be used for other applications, combined with other datasets, and, ultimately, a monetizable asset in and of itself.

With multiple datasets becoming available from various connected machines, enterprises and their data scientists have been able develop substantially bigger pictures of the equipment, including wider reaching processing and analysis of the data. As this data has increased in scale, speed, and structure, and as enterprises have developed and applied advanced analytical tools and machine learning, the outcomes of data processing have become even more promising.

New insights, based on, for example, predictive maintenance, fraud detection, and condition monitoring have moved the goalposts from describing *how things are* to *what could happen*, and allow for enterprises to take preventive action. This preventive action, in turn, can save industries millions of dollars in terms of minimized operational disruptions, improved machine efficiency, productivity, and early detection of faults and fraud.

Consider the following examples. Within most industries, maintenance routines are either based on defined schedules or some method of condition based monitoring. Operators of, for example, wind turbines or rolling stock would carry out maintenance routines per set schedules, and in many cases, this was irrespective of whether the equipment actually required the routine service. While routines have helped structure unplanned disruptions into predicted activities, with connected machinery, enterprises monitor in real-time the operational performance of machines, and with the assistance of advanced analytics, predict with greater degrees of accuracy when maintenance is required. Particularly, the ability to aggregate and analyze data from multiple sensors such as temperature, vibration, noise, and images has enhanced the ability to detect future faults with greater accuracy.

What applications such as predictive maintenance, fraud detection, and condition monitoring bring to IoT and enterprises is a greater efficiency and productivity to operational performance. This development is a step further on from monitoring and remote control and management, and involves additional tools such as advanced analytics and machine learning. These continue to improve with more and more domain expertise becoming involved in the development of these tools.

Automation

Manufacturing industries have followed developments from early M2M to current stages in IoT, including monitoring, remote control, management, efficiencies, and productivity. Recently, a manufacturing executive expressed the next goal as being to remove "the security risks in operations by operators."

In high-volume, high-speed production environments, real-time, and near instantaneous decision-making has become a critical component in manufacturing environments. With analytical tools able to ingest, process, and analyze substantial amounts of data in real-time, the goal of full automation within operations is coming closer and closer within reach of manufacturers. Based on operational performance data and prescriptive analytics, and driven by such significant initiatives as Industrie 4.0 in Germany, Smart Manufacturing at GE in the US, and many innovation centers in Japan, Europe, and China, the goal is to achieve operational efficiency and productivity through automation.

Closed-loop improvements

The benefits and opportunities outlined in monitoring, remote control and management capabilities, efficiency and productivity mechanisms, and ultimately, automation share one common feature as described here. They are all based on what may be termed closed-loop improvements or services where data from connected devices is used to optimize operational performance.

Vendors have provided many of these services in the past although none have benefitted from real-time data originating directly from the connected equipment or machinery. This combination of real-time data, ideally from multiple sources to strengthen the analytical processing power, has enabled enterprises to move onto the next stages of analytical outcomes—from descriptive to predictive and prescriptive output.

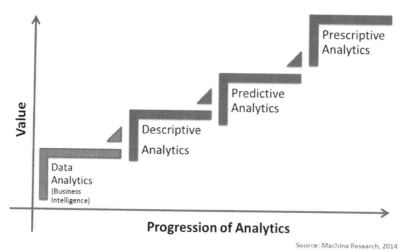

FIGURE 2.2: Progression of analytic outcomes [Source: Machina Research, 2016]

The shift in analytic outcomes from looking and analyzing the past to looking at the future has been made possible by this growing amount data, analytical tools, and continued developments in analytical processes. A brief description of each analytical outcome may help.

Diagnostic analytics and Business Intelligence

Business intelligence (BI) refers to "...a variety of software applications used to analyze an organization's raw data. BI as a discipline is made up of several related activities, including data mining, online analytical processing, querying and reporting."[8] Business intelligence differs from the following analytics techniques, including diagnostic analytics, in that BI has always played a key role in the strategic planning process of an enterprise, and not as part of the actual operational processes—which has been the role of diagnostic analytics. BI allows enterprises to gather, store, access and analyze data to assist and enhance their decision-making processes. It is with the emergence of data from connected devices that these new analytical techniques have started to deliver additional value.

Descriptive analytics

Descriptive analytics involves the analysis of data to summarize what happened in a particular event. This is the objective of most analytical approaches currently followed by enterprises. The output provides information, such as performance data, relationships between datasets, and information about the status and condition of items of machinery.

Predictive analytics

Predictive analytics has emerged as the next step in the progression. Predictive analytics includes a variety of processing and analytical tools to prepare and analyze data, and deliver insights relating to anticipated outcomes. Predictive analytics makes use of both historical and recent data as well as analytical tools such as machine learning, advanced algorithms, modeling, and data mining. Here, the focus shifts from what has happened to what may happen.

---

8 For more information, see Business Intelligence Definition and Solutions, http://www.cio.com/article/2439504/business-intelligence/business-intelligence-definition-andsolutions.

The primary objective is to predict future outcomes from known data; one key example is predictive maintenance, but other applications include predictive policing, predictive health-care or predictive movement (i.e., pedestrian, cyclist, and vehicular traffic). In the case of descriptive and predictive analytics, the analysis is carried out on predominantly enterprise-owned or enterprise-managed data.

The enterprise captures, processes, and owns most enterprise data analyzed. However, some predictive analytics solutions have started to include external data, although the scope remains limited and mainly involves so-called open data made public by government bodies. For an interesting overview of what has become publicly available in terms of open data, explore the 100 civic datasets released at the end of 2014 by Bristol City Council, the Future Cities Catapult and the Connected Digital Economy Catapult.[9]

Prescriptive analytics

Prescriptive analytics is next. This enables enterprises to move beyond basic data analysis and outcome prediction to a new level of analytical insight where actions are defined and potentially implemented or executed autonomously (i.e., with cyber-physical systems defining and evaluating their own decisions and acting upon them).

Prescriptive analytics builds on predictive analytics, by not only presenting the predicted outcome but also suggesting a range of possible actions. Each action in turn is analyzed and risk-weighted in a way that, in very simple terms, resembles human thought process.

This analytical approach starts off by assessing the impact of actions, using this assessment of future scenarios to determine the best option. The process can also be highly sensitive

9 See Digital Catapult Centre, "New Open Data Collaboration to Help Bristolians Find Value in their Data" July 3, 2014, https://www. digitalcatapultcentre.org.uk/new-open-data-collaboration-to-help-bristolians-find-value-intheir-data/.

to real-time data, constantly reviewing and assessing the next action, which in turn may be equally time-sensitive and play an integral part in deciding the subsequent course.

The connected car is a good example of the full spectrum of analytic objectives. Sharing information about the car's speed, location, fuel levels, and so on are examples of descriptive analytics, visualized mainly on dashboards. Within this category, flagging maintenance and service routines is also part of descriptive analytics. The analysis of this data leads to predictive analytics, such as data warning of impending brake failures or engine data showing signs of potential cracks in the combustion block.

Finally, prescriptive analytics come in with self-driving vehicles that accumulate significant amounts of real-time data to control and direct the vehicle's self-driving operation, providing a safe and comfortable journey from A to B with limited human intervention. What is important about prescriptive analytics, significantly different from descriptive and predictive analytics, is that external enterprise data is judged as integral in achieving the appropriate levels of prescription. It is here that we need to begin to talk about Operational Data Spaces.

The next evolution: Operational Data Spaces

Before discussing Operational Data Spaces, it is important to make the distinction between enterprise internal and external data. Enterprises will quickly recognize internal data when defined as that data either managed through existing legacy, enterprise systems such as Enterprise Resource Planning (ERP), Customer Relationship Management (CRM), and Sales Force Automation solutions, or generated as part of the operations and activities of the enterprise business. This will include everything from production data, to financial data, to customer data, and product performance and usage data, obtained through connected devices. Ultimately there is no definitive border as to what constitutes internal data, as enterprise internal data may extend from data within a department to a business unit, and to data within entire business entities within or at the corporate level itself.

External data encompasses enterprise data sources that are outside of the operational and business activities of the enterprise. The range of external data sources is immense and can include everything from open data sources offered by governmental institutions, to traffic information, weather information, location information, social media data, industry statistics, and so on. External data may also include other enterprises within the same industry segments which—through open data collaboration—could significantly enhance operations within the given industry.

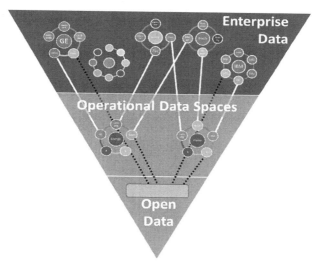

FIGURE 2.3: Three categories of data in a 'System of Systems' world
[Source: Machina Research, 2016]

It is at the point of aggregation of internal and external data that innovative and unique insights may be achieved by enterprises through processing and analysis. While aggregating internal and external data does open several issues around data security and potentially data privacy and ownership, it is expected that as use and data frameworks evolve, so too will the safeguards and policies around data security, privacy, and ownership.

Where are we with closed-loop services?

Closed-loop services have delivered tremendous benefits in M2M and IoT. Through smarter, connected devices, advanced analytics, and a greater range of analytic outcomes, vendors could extend services around their products. As illustrated in Figure 2.4: Multiple single closed-loop services by multiple vendors [Source: Machina Research, 2016]2.4, vendors have provided enterprises with point-to-point M2M and IoT solutions, creating multiple single "siloed" solutions with enterprise data managed in a highly decentralized and ungoverned way.

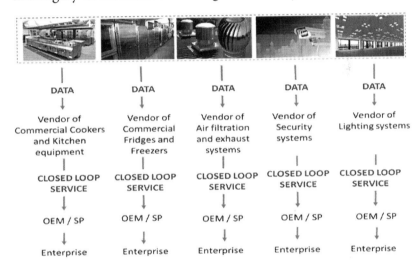

FIGURE 2.4: Multiple single closed-loop services by multiple vendors
[Source: Machina Research, 2016]

Closed-loop services have remained firmly focused on enterprise data, i.e. internal data, and with very little openness around the sharing of data. Only when enterprises began to explore prescriptive analytics or further develop analytical processes has the aggregation and augmentation of internal enterprise data with external data become important.

It is at this very point that enterprises have started to recognize the need to look and manage beyond the closed-loop environments, and explore, how external data can be introduced to their systems, and equally important, how internal data can be securely and appropriately managed in this "system of systems."[10]

This shift reflects the change from a product-centric IoT approach to more of a data-centric one. The remainder of our book focuses on the limitations of the closed-loop service and the possibilities for enterprises that can be realized though a well-considered deployment architecture.

10 For further discussion on "system of systems," read Michael E. Porter and James E. Heppelmann's "How Smart, Connected Products Are Transforming Competition," in Harvard Business Review, November 2014 issue.

Chapter 3

Contemplating Big Data in IoT and the Predictive Era

Big Data is a fortuitous confluence of circumstances.

One thing is certain: IoT will be responsible for a vast increase in the amount of data for almost everyone. While sharp disagreements exist in the IoT world about many topics, there is little disagreement on this. Commonly referred to as "big data" in the industry, the narrative about this has been continuously shaped since 2011. It is worthwhile to examine IoT in the context of this narrative, looking at the key elements of volume, variety, and velocity.

Volume

Our ancestors knew the value of storing data, information, and knowledge, but goodness how expensive it was! What we might call "modern" papermaking techniques evolved in perhaps the second century BCE in Ancient China but the real step-changes in information storage might be dated to the fifteenth century with Johannes Gutenberg's printing press, and, of course, to the development of magnetic techniques of storing data in the twentieth century. Since just 1980, we've seen the cost of storing a single gigabyte of data drop from \$1M to around three cents.

This precipitous drop in the cost of storage was, of course, not enough to make big data meaningful. It's a mistake to think big data is just about storing information. Information stored but never used is a lot like having a million tons of broccoli-flavored cotton candy; it takes up a lot of space and doesn't have much value.

In parallel to the drop is storage costs, we've seen a drastic reduction in the cost of computation, usually measured in floating point operations per second, or FLOPS. Today we commonly measure in GigaFLOPS (10^9 FLOPS), though computers exist that measure their computing capacity in TeraFLOPS (10^{12} FLOPS). It's estimated that since 1960 we've seen this cost per GigaFLOP drop from \$146B to just about eight cents!

This massive evolution of computing and storage power has yielded a plethora of new frameworks for parallel processing of data. Often when we speak of big data, we mean Hadoop, Spark, and related tools. Distributed computing frameworks like this have opened an entire world of data science previously unavailable to all, but the largest organizations and governments. It is this fortuitous confluence of circumstances that led to companies storing more data, which, in turn, led to improvements in data science and applied mathematics justifying further storage of data, starting the positive feedback cycle we find ourselves in today.

Variety

In the early days of the computing era, computing was a field dominated by mathematicians, physicists, and other practitioners of esoteric and highly specialized knowledge. They dealt almost exclusively with numerical data but as computers have entered our homes, and our pockets (smart phones), cars (connected cars), and, indeed, our mouths (Bluetooth toothbrushes), the variety of data has blossomed to include textual, audio, video, and spatial data. We certainly still apply mathematical techniques in our analysis, but the data isn't readily amenable to the standard data structures like matrices without considerable data engineering. Fortunately, computer scientists have developed a range of tools for handling that data, numericizing and performing computations on it so we can infer human intention by analyzing such things as the forms of spelling in our tweets and the landscape of our Instagram posts.

Velocity

The racing driver Mario Andretti once said, "If everything seems under control, you're just not going fast enough." He could have been talking about the rush towards ever faster data for which we are still evolving analysis capabilities. The financial markets are an obvious illustration of this, where trading has moved from the floor traders on exchanges to computer-based, ultra-high frequency trading where a given trader might be in and out of over a hundred trades in less than a second. Some of this high-speed data is easier to understand than others, which creates opportunities as well as peril, as we have also seen by the financial markets. This will be true for IoT as well. The speed of data being absorbed across a broad array of sensors will create new opportunities for adaptive systems.

Our dearth of analysis techniques notwithstanding, the hardware and software that drive our world are now entirely capable of capturing and communicating all this data at high speed and low latency ("real-time"), and this is particularly interesting in burgeoning IoT subspecialties, such as transportation and logistics.

The 5 Cs of IoT

With big data in mind, it is useful to then dive deeper into the elements of IoT to understand the implications.

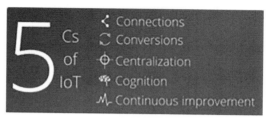

FIGURE 3.1

Smart <u>c</u>onnections: This encompasses the sensors and communication systems that capture data, moving it from the physical world to the cyber world. From the world we can see, hear, smell, touch, and taste to a world we can synthesize and analyze at computer's mind-bending speeds. Because so much of the world is becoming connected, the amount of data will continue to grow at a massive pace.

Data to information <u>c</u>onversions: This generally contemplates data blending and simple computation such as conditional (IF-THEN-ELSE) statements. Often this type of calculation is also well suited to be performed "at the edge" or near the source of the data.

Let us imagine a simple device many of us have in our homes today, a thermostat which drives heating and cooling systems to keep the indoor temperature at a desirable level.

A modern digital version of this device has a sensor, which determines the temperature perhaps as many as 12,000 times per second (12,000 Hz). Many applications of this sensor may warrant such high velocity data but certainly not this particular use-case, therefore some basic data filtering is appropriate. The basic analysis would be something as simple as "IF <current temperature> EQUALS <previous temperature> THEN <don't transmit the data>."

We still don't have *information*; it's just raw data. This only becomes information once we blend it with other raw data such as:

- What is the commanded temperature setting (system status from a sensor)?

- Are heating/cooling systems already operating and if so, at what intensity (yet another sensor)?
- Which heating/cooling commands are necessary to achieve the desired temperature in the required time-frame (static lookup table)?

One of the key shifts the market will see is the architecture required to truly leverage the data. That is the fundamental thesis of this book. We certainly may want to share this raw data and outcome data in a manner that allows for multiple constituents to use it for a variety of purposes. That said, for the purposes of keeping the temperature comfortable, the edge device can and should be configured to process these messages and take the appropriate action. In this case, the edge device can be the thermostat itself.

Centralization: What we've come to know as a data lake stems from a term coined by Pentaho's CTO, James Dixon. Far from suggesting a monolithic disk and supercomputer, the idea is that data and information are propagated from the various silos to permit blending-at-scale, aggregating across space and time while taking advantage of the cost-efficient computational capabilities, like those provided by Hadoop or Spark and similar distributed computing frameworks.

Initially, the platforms used for this had simple data on-boarding and computational frameworks but with the dramatic reduction in costs and complexity, the industry has seen the capabilities evolve significantly. Where previously organizations would only consider such platforms for batch processing, usually of analytical queries, now they can service data-in-motion, data-at-rest, analytical queries, self-service data, reporting, machine learning, and much more. The ideal state in the short-term is that these systems are increasingly becoming sufficiently data-aware to the point that many people and organizations no longer view a distributed computing platform as any different than other architectures.

In the past, there has been a strong and widespread desire

to have data stored in file systems that were ACID compliant. "ACID" stands for atomicity, concurrency, isolation, and durability. Given the nature of the available computing and storage, until the mid to late 2000s, few applications needed the type of scale, flexibility, or distributed characteristics that would make ACID compliance an issue, so few organizations would have even thought to question this approach. But as the processing continued to be greater in power and at a lower cost, and storage kept getting cheaper and cheaper, the market began to see the rise of NoSQL databases like Hadoop and Cassandra and MongoDB and others, which were designed to be highly distributed and highly resilient, but relaxed some of the ACID requirements. So large scale applications, especially ones that were online and mobile applications like Facebook and other social media sites began to build their solutions around the idea of eventual consistency, which among other things, accommodated scale in a much more cost effective way. As opposed to ACID, this approach is referred to as BASE (basically available, soft state, eventually consistent).

Being able to access the sensor data, transform it, and propagate it to a central repository is key to an organization's ability to drive value from the data. But it should be noted that the right architecture does not restrict the propagation of data to one and only one repository. The same data collected once, using the right architecture, can be leveraged by multiple central repositories (like the organization that is using the IoT subsystem, the organization that markets the IoT subsystem, the third parties that work with the organization using the subsystem, the regulatory agencies concerned with that organization, and more. And the central repositories of one may be combining that data with other sources that look nothing like the other user's repositories, but the ability to combine and analyze this data is at the heart of where value is driven from IoT.

Cognition: "It's not what you look at that matters, it's what you see," wrote poet Henry David Thoreau. The "second C" was about transforming data into information. This "fourth C" is about deriving knowledge from information. Knowledge can mean many things, such as the insight gained from the capability to detect a departure from normal conditions (as in unsupervised learning) or predict real world outcomes (supervised learning). It is the realm of advanced operational, investigative, and predictive analytics, as well as machine learning, data science, and artificial intelligence.

The computational complexity of the algorithms and their hunger for data is such that our previous step of building the data lake provides an ideal platform for performing these operations.

The reduction of data silos yields the ability to ask more complex questions such as:

- Is my factory's energy consumption anomalous when compared to similar factories with similar needs in similar climates?
- If not, what's likely the problem?

The more data that exists, sometimes seemingly unrelated, the more granular the signature of that data and the deeper the analysis can be. Of course, this is a relatively trivial case of the type basic "IoT" infrastructure in the market in the last few years can accomplish with relative ease. The real challenges come in far more complex cases involving thousands if not tens-of-thousands of data dimensions with trillions of data points. At that level, simple aggregation and nineteenth century linear regression techniques (the work-horse of modern statistical analysis) fail to provide much insight.

Continuous improvement: In some ways, this is the key to IoT. With sensors constantly collecting data and the computational capabilities associated with processing that data, the ability exists (and will continue to become more sophisticated) to utilize machine learning techniques to create truly adaptive systems. By doing this, organization are using operational transformation and moving the insight gained from the cyber world back to the physical one. In most cases, the predictions gleaned from the combined efforts of our previous four Cs will not be sufficient to realize tangible benefits. Most would likely believe today that the thought of being in a self-driving car, lacking a steering wheel and pedals as a backup system, makes them uneasy. The technology is there, but the human condition suggests a reluctance to let go of what's known and provides comfort. But that will change.

The Dawn of the Predictive Era

Computing is evolving. It's likely that the forces described by Moore's Law and Dennard Scaling will mean that many of the ideas we've associated with technological advancement will change. It won't be about faster, cheaper, and smaller computers in the year 2025; prediction and where we apply it will be the big story.

Most readers will be old enough to remember what photography was like in 1995. We bought film, took photos, and hoped for the best when we dropped our handiwork off to be developed. The idea of taking twenty snaps of the same subject in the hope of getting a single good shot was a luxury only professionals could afford. Photography was fundamentally a chemical engineering problem, and an expensive one at that.

Today disks are larger and cheaper, LCDs and monitors are far more advanced, and printers can do the job previously restricted to professional photography studios. What was fundamentally a chemical engineering problem was reframed as a home computing one—and this was driven by the dramatic reduction in computing technology prices.

Similar forces are at work when it comes to prediction. As computation and storage costs fall over the next decade and techniques, like machine learning rapidly improve, we'll see the predictive "toolbox" be applied in ways never before seen. Just a few years ago, the only place we could consider self-driving cars was in a highly controlled environment like a warehouse where we could program every possible scenario deterministically (not predictively).

Today the ability to make accurate predictions means that

self-driving cars are being tested in "normal" environments that include pedestrians, drunk drivers, and damaged road signs. Problems that had to be solved using "brute-force" can now be tactically solved in a probabilistic (predictive) manner. As the cost of prediction continues to plummet, it will be applied in increasingly new places and at a much higher scale.

Why Now? The Rule of Threes!

First, many of the mathematical techniques required to make prediction possible really kicked off in the seventies, as artificial neural networks advanced along with better methods of training them.

Second, the availability of unlimited and virtually free storage, compute, and communications infrastructure in the form of cloud computing makes the mathematics previously mentioned computationally feasible and moves them from theory into practice. What was once possible but impractical has become affordable and accessible, and thus practical. This is the key imperative in moving any technology from the laboratory into the mainstream.

The third, and perhaps most visible for those on the frontline of corporate technology, is the diminishing return on ERP investment. Simply capturing data and streamlining business process workflows yielded enormous benefits over the last decades, but while many ERP systems are still in use today in a vast number of organizations, their ability to drive competitive differentiation is being challenged. We've reached a new steady state where effective ERP implementation is so prevalent, as not to be a key differentiator.

The implications of increased sophistication in predictive analytics, the affordability of computing resources needed to scale such analysis, and the need to move beyond ERP systems is creating the "predictive era." In this, the ability to on-board data, perform feature engineering (data engineering), train predictive models, and deploy/orchestrate those models is becoming a core competency for every business. Along with new applications for predictive analytics, organizations will benefit from greater returns on complementary skills, such as data science.

This sets an important stage. The evolution of technology is painfully clear on so many levels, enabling new and exciting opportunities. The massive emphasis on big data, including the corresponding technology retooling of many organizations is an unmistakable indication that these organizations appreciate the significant value that lies in the data. The question now becomes "What will organizations do to truly leverage data in an IoT world"? And with this, we begin our exploration.

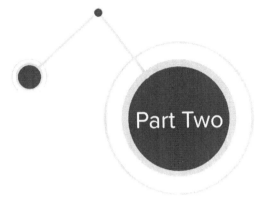

Part Two

The Fundamental Flaws in Where We Are Today

"The breathtaking view at the mountaintop is compensation for all of the breath lost whilst sweating towards it."
–Matshona Dhliwayo

The Limitations of Early IoT Systems

In the coming year or two, IoT focus will become much more holistic, shifting from a simpler message-response view to an emphasis on the utility value of the data. Both the driverless car and the wired Coke machine represent compelling factors of IoT. While technologically possible today, due to overwhelming regulatory and infrastructure challenges, driverless cars aren't yet an everyday reality. In other words, it's possible, but not practical. The instrumented coke machine, on the other hand, is very real. Most people think this machine "phones home" when it needs to be refilled or alert a service technician the temperature is too high or too low. In a sense, this is true. These are message-response systems, where messages trigger corresponding responses. These are communicated in "if then, then that" terms, and, potentially, they save a lot of money and provide value.

What we should expect the market to see in the next year is a much greater emphasis on the underlying machine or sensor data. This isn't at the expense of message-response systems, quite the contrary. The "execution engine" in message-response systems tells the system what to do under certain conditions.

As more and more IoT data is collected, greater knowledge can be derived from that data. Moreover, the Holy Grail may well be the "utility value of the data," where cleansed and enriched data coming from not one, but many closed-loop systems, as well as external non-IoT data, can be cleansed and combined to find much deeper meaning via the correlation of data and the emergent patterns that might otherwise be hidden. Therefore, expect the role of and focus on the data within IoT will become prominent in 2017 and beyond.

To date, the systems, while increasing in functionality, as well as underlying system management and industrial strength capabilities, have had their fair share of limitations, and it is worthwhile to take stock in those limitations in the context of understanding the likely, or desirable path forward.

IoT for the sake of IoT: lack of practical usefulness

With any meaningful market progression, hype breeds greed, innovation, opportunity, and sometimes ideas that may be really creative, but somewhat lacking in usefulness, in part, out of pure excitement to exploit the technology. This isn't altogether bad. We learn from success and failure, but it may undermine the acceptance of this technology, in some instances, because it rightfully calls product usefulness into question.

It is one thing for a product to lack control or to have limited, yet compelling functionality. It is another thing altogether to have IoT-enabled devices that simply do not seem to make any sense to the average person. While it is inevitable in any strong phase of technology, some will believe tying anything to the wave makes sense. Just as we saw with the Internet boom in the late nineties, not everything applies to the wave. Sometimes the IoT-enabled device may not truly need to be IoT-enabled. While IoT technology is exciting, that doesn't suggest that every single object needs to be IoT-enabled.

For example, a Bluetooth-enabled, programmable LED dog collar isn't probably on your must-have list of devices. The people making the Neopop device[11] probably disagree, as they

---

11 https://www.cnet.com/news/light-up-your-pets-with-thi
s-neopop-led-collar/.

felt the need to produce such a device. For starters, the standard information you want on your dog's collar is where the dog belongs, namely, your home. If your dog is lost, then it is likely not in range for Bluetooth connectivity, and therefore, there's no way to change the message, although you probably wouldn't want to anyway, because if the dog is lost, the key message is probably where to return it, which is typically found on a standard, non-Bluetooth collar. Give the Neopop team an A for creativity.-

Sometimes, brilliant products begin with either failures or efforts with only marginal success. The category of products with questionable usefulness is an interesting lens into product vision, because what might have been labeled as senseless or meaningless may be the early (and poor) version of something, with the proper augmentation and delivery considerations, that might actually become valuable, even mainstream.

One example of this is the smart refrigerator. At first glance, having a refrigerator that's smart had a bunch of limitations. The idea that you would have to log items as you put then in your refrigerator via a screen seemed unlikely. For a function to be useful, it must be incredibly easy, or it won't be used. Cameras on the inside and outside of the door can be used for bar code scanning and make this much easier. That only goes so far, though, because things like fruit or deli meat generally don't have barcodes, although even this is changing. But this speaks to the early days of the Internet of Things, and in particular, the limitations we have now been able to see, and learn from, as they began to enter the market. Smart refrigerators will continue to evolve and change based on market pressures to a point where they are indeed quite useful.

Compelling but limited features

Many of the early IoT systems had a compelling factor associated with them—yet those features were fundamentally limited. This was more on display in the consumer market than those systems aimed commercially, but it also makes sense that the early instances would also be limited in commercial products as well. This isn't a criticism (although accounting for some of these may unavoidably seem that way), but rather a somewhat natural and expected scenario. One thing is for sure, the "compelling" was enough, in many cases, to overcome the "limited," at least for a while.

Consumer markets have a particularly large number of examples. For instance, there is the Quirky Smart Egg Tray. With this device, you can know the number of eggs in your refrigerator by checking your phone. This isn't a system, nor is it a complex application, but rather an application where the sensors in the egg tray are linked directly to the application that lets you know how many eggs you have. So in the context of knowing how many eggs you have, that's somewhat compelling. That is, until you stop and consider that you can generally open the door of the refrigerator and see how many eggs you have. Granted, you need to do that before going to the grocery store, but it's not like you must do anything that takes more than three seconds or have the mental capacity of a puppy.

There's the smart water fountain for cats. This device keeps tabs on your cat's water intake. It is a product from Pura Cat. If you are away from home a lot and want to better understand your cat's water consumption, this will do it for you. This is an interesting illustration in that what you get here, while very limited in capabilities, is a more granular understanding of a given condition. You could check the water intake of your cat the old fashion way, namely, look at the bowl and take note of how much water the cat had during the day. To better understand when and how much water your cat is drinking, this device offers a more granular signature. An obvious question is why you'd need or want such insight.

Do you grill? Perhaps you invested in a Green Egg. If so, you may also have an Internet-connected smart grill. With this, you can monitor and adjust the temperature, grilling time, and turn the grill on and off. This is pretty compelling. You put the tender-loin on the grill, then catch the beginning of the third quarter of the football game while glancing at your phone to see if you need to head back out again. But you get what you get, literally. Not unlike many other applications, at least at first, it's fairly limited in what it does. This has downstream potential for sure, and is, by all accounts, a somewhat more logical implementation of an IoT product.

There are smart blinds that can be controlled remotely by your phone, and even programmed to go up and down with sunrise and sunset, or other prescribed times. Some might say this is automating what doesn't need automation. There's an advertisement where the husband comes home and complains to his wife that he tried to turn the TV on with the remote and the "blinds went up." He's dumbfounded. His wife explains smart blinds, to which he responds, "You're a genius." Perhaps. The counterargument here is smart blinds will evolve beyond "compelling, but limited" capabilities Smart blinds are natural candidates to be integrated into a product system.

The potential for smart blinds is likely better than the potential for the Belty, which is an Internet-connected belt that automatically loosens based on the pressure against it. So you eat too much for dinner, and your belt adjusts. One could argue the value of eating too much, then seeing this reflected on your phone is negligible, since you are, after all, wearing the belt. The sensory perception is likely to be more informative than the alert on your phone.

As if to highlight the idea of "compelling but limited" features, the follow-up version of this belt boasts a buckle that looks more like what someone might actually wear, and also interacts with companion apps, like one that monitors activity and hydration. Is this better? In some ways, the integration and additional information is a step in the right direction, but for $395, it is hard to imagine this product will be flying off the shelves.

One of the epicenters of compelling but limited (and arguably unnecessary) products is the kitchen. Take the Pantelligent smart frying pan.[12] This tells you the temperature in the frying pan. And because it can link, via Bluetooth, to your phone, it can tell you when the pan is too hot or not hot enough, and if you punch in what it is you're cooking, your phone can tell you when to flip the salmon or whatever it is you're making.

Do you have a cocktail with dinner? Then perhaps you'll want to use a Bluetooth enabled cocktail shaker. It is "equipped with a high-precision weight sensor, a set of accelerometers, and a Bluetooth radio that allows it to relay data to your smart-phone."[13] Now the first and clearly obvious question is why the app from the app store you get for free, or the incredible one for $2.99 doesn't serve the same purpose. They all give you the amounts, so the weight sensors might not be critical. They tell whether you need to shake or stir, and some might go so far as to tell you to "shake vigorously," so paying $89 to $159 for the shaker that's connected to your phone may be overkill.

After dinner, you might be up for a nice cup of tea from your iKettle.[14] An age-old consensus holds that the most basic task in cooking is to boil water, and that someone who "can't boil water" has no business being in a kitchen. But with an iKettle, a smart phone, Wi-Fi connectivity, and the time to configure and install a smart kettle, you can now pre-program your kettle to boil water at a certain time or simply be notified it is boiling without having to stand there and wait. In fact, looking at the Smarter (the company that sells the iKettle) website, they pose the question, "What will you do with all your spare time?" that you ostensibly otherwise lose by not using an iKettle. This might be less "compelling" and more "limited."

The kitchen isn't the only place where these products appear. A walk down the hallway to the bedroom reveals more examples.

---

12 https://www.pantelligent.com/how-it-works/.

13 http://www.digitaltrends.com/home/b4rm4n-barman-smart-cocktail-shaker-kickstarter/.

14 http://smarter.am/ikettle/#.

There's the Perseus mirror,[15] which many may likely believe are very compelling. While one could argue it's basically a large iPhone screen that's a part of a bathroom mirror, the counterargument is it's true. When you are at the mirror in the morning getting ready for work, what do you think about? Do you ponder your day's schedule? Do you consider the weather? Do you care about the news? Are you wondering if you got that important email you were waiting for? It isn't uncommon for people to be interacting with their phones in the morning for all the above reasons. Is taking such information and presenting it on your mirror a must-have? Probably not. But for many, it might be thought of as compelling.

The downstream possibilities here, ranging from a more interactive interface to greater content depth, all of which are sure to happen, are intriguing and speak to the evolution (and integration characteristics) of the Internet of Things. A bigger leap, however, is found in the Smartress Lover Detection System.[16] This mattress allows you to understand when the mattress is in use and the pattern of the movement on the mattress. Some might say "compelling but limited" features. Others might characterize this in other terms. Those trying to rationalize paranoia might suggest this has genuine value in assisting with sleep patterns. Okay, but you can get a free app that works by laying your phone under your pillow that does the same thing.

There are many, many other examples. If you think back to the tech bubble, companies that were basic product companies started changing their names to add ".com" with the belief that having a website that made their product literature available online increased their value. When it became clear they had to sell their products online, that ruled some out, but those who doubled down by doing so were clearly betting on the palpable hype of the Internet boom.

The same might be said for smart connected products. It's

---

15 http://www.perseusmirrors.com.
16 http://www.smarttress.com/en.

one thing to sell a widget. And perhaps in the past decade or so, you put a microchip into the widget you make and you offer it as a "smart widget," like say, a kettle. Generally speaking, the "smart widgets" were more expensive, but not by much, and generally brought added value to the product by what made it smart. In the case of the kettle, you could program it to start heating the water four minutes before your alarm went off, so you could wake up, walk to the kitchen, and pour your tea. All good.

Now the idea that smart products are becoming smart connected products makes great sense in many cases. But there seems to be near hysteria around the idea that the progression to smart connected products is some holy grail. So like the craziness we all observed with the Internet boom, we are now seeing a bit of it with smart connected products.

In 2013, Procter and Gamble introduced the TweetPee,[17] which is an insert you put into your baby's diaper to notify you when you need to change it (although as of now, it appears to be only available in Portuguese). To their credit (and benefit), they are also allowing you to link it to your diaper inventory, so you also get notifications to replenish. Crisis averted, at least in Lisbon.

Then there is a fork called the HapiFork[18] (by Hapilabs) that tracks your eating rate. Although there are limitations as to how you use the fork, you get the data they determine you should receive, which isn't at all uncommon with any new, more limited IoT-enabled product. It provides coaching as to how to eat, and has red and green lights on the fork. This, again, might be viewed as compelling but limited, but it is a lens into where we're headed. The instrumentation will continue to get smaller, so the fork today (which arguably looks like a baby's first fork) will give way to a fork that looks more in keeping with what you would expect, not unlike the second version of the Belty. And too, the cost will continue to drop, making products that provide very

17 https://www.cnet.com/news/tweetpee-huggies-sends-a-tweet-when-babys-wet/.

18 https://www.hapi.com/product/hapifork

little additional value at an-all-but-unaffordable cost evolve to the point where the marginal cost comes down dramatically and the added value climbs.

Some of smart connected products will evolve to the point of mainstream relevance, and others (many) will die before getting there. At issue will be the extent to which prices fall, value goes up, and that value is seen in the context of a broader "Product System."

The "Product System" is a logical extension of these underlying smart connected products, where the value is increased by coexisting with other smart connected products. Take the Samsung "Family Hub" Smart Refrigerator.[19] There's been a fair amount of criticism since its introduction to the market.[20] The idea is that the refrigerator is the place the family converges. When we were growing up, the door of the fridge is where we'd post candid photos, the grocery list, along with a reminder the school play was Thursday.

Now we're in the digital age. Why not recreate this and more, with the refrigerator as the digital hub? Some legitimate questions are raised. For instance, for the incremental money you spend on this (the Family Hub fridge starts at $5799), couldn't you have a more powerful tablet in the kitchen performing these functions better, with more apps and connectivity, and that's far cheaper? And too, the refrigerator is meant to last a decade or more, but that life span would be ridiculous for the tablet, so why constrain yourself by a lock-in that doesn't seem remotely sensible? And yet, the compelling features are just that, compelling features. The cameras, there are three, allow you to see what's in your fridge from your phone, so you can check it from the grocery store. There are apps that assign expiration dates.

While somewhat limited, the frig shows value in the combination of technologies and data that can come together. The "hub" needs to be more than a place photos and recipes are found. It's

19 http://www.samsung.com/us/explore/family-hub-refrigerator/.
20 http://www.theverge.com/circuitbreaker/2016/5/4/11591780/ samsung-family-hub-smart-fridge-hands-on-price-release-date.

the architecture and corresponding products that connect other products and gather data across the ecosystem to derive greater value, both in how any single product operates, as well as the collective insight gained from the aggregation of data. Such data can now be understood in the context of the other products. Are they coming together in a somewhat clunky and overpriced way? Perhaps. Still, credit is due Samsung for taking the bluster and rhetoric around IoT and doing something that will foreshadow the overall direction of the market.

Fitbits[21] have been around for a while. The early ones were, like most IoT-enabled products, very limited in what they could do. Over time, the ability to link them to other apps, to measure more from the product itself (heart rate, for instance), and to see more information has progressed. Yet, you are still basically relegated to see what Fitbit wants you to see. Your control of the data is limited. Still, the linkages to other applications become table stakes for staying relevant. This is true of all fitness trackers and now, smart watches (which you can also get from Fitbit). And this points to a time in the future where the utility value of the underlying data collected by the Fitbit will be far greater than the limited value derived by your ability to see your heart rate or know how many steps you took today.

The home is probably an even better example. Notwithstanding the silliness of the smart forks and kitty water dishes, there are several smart connected products in the home that are beginning to work together, and this will only continue. Groups like the Allseen Alliance have worked to get the industry pointed towards interconnectivity standards and greater coalescence of smart connected products into a "product system" we will call a "smart home."

We have been talking about smart homes for years, and the players involved have been around for sometime, including those who came and went. For instance, Revolv[22] was targeted to be the

21 https://en.wikipedia.org/wiki/Fitbit.
22 http://www.zdnet.com/article/revolv-is-dead-google-killed-i
t-long-live-innovation/.

smart home hub, connecting a variety of devices in the home and reconciling some of the issues associated with controlling and connecting disparate products. Revolv was funded by Tech Stars in 2012 as MobiPlug, and changed its name to Revolv in 2013. But Google Nest acquired Revolv in 2014, and it was subsequently shut down, much to the chagrin of those who purchased the lifetime warranty.

But the playing field remains robust.[23] Google Nest, Apple Homekit, and Samsung SmartThings all have major initiatives to own this market, connecting a variety of products into a seamless ecosystem. And not to be left out, Amazon has entered the fray with Echo, offering another option for connecting your smart home.

And what specific products are we talking about? A lot, to be sure. There are smart doorbells and smart door (and other) locks by a variety of players. Some are new on the scene, like August,[24], and some have been in the door lock business for years but now have smart connected product offerings, like Schlage.[25] These products all have the need to connect into your smart home hub, and the market has progressed to a point where everyone is beginning to expect interconnectivity and common integrated control.

The same is true for smart lights, like CREE or the Phillips Hue. These will cost a fortune, but last so much longer and do so much more. For instance, you can exploit programmable links to direct the lights to change color when certain conditions occur, like a message from one of your kids or a new Twitter follower.

Lack of control

Most of the early IoT-enabled products provided compelling capabilities that were explicitly limited to what the product providers wanted the users to have, where the control was also explicitly limited to the capabilities provided by the supplier.

23 http://appcarousel.com/the-battle-to-become-the-center-of-your-connected-home-insights-from-ces/.
24 http://august.com/products/august-doorbell/.
25 http://www.schlage.com/en/home/keyless-deadbolt-locks/connect.html.

This isn't surprising, but as we will see moving forward, users will demand increasing control over the capabilities of both the operation of the products and, perhaps especially, the leverage of the data.

In a closed-loop, message-response system represented by most of the early IoT products, the sensors in the product are directly tied to the consuming application. So, the sensors in the fitness tracker, for instance, are consumed by the tracking application. The device might be tracking steps, miles, and stairs. There isn't all that much to work with when the device itself is narrowly scoped. The display, also limited, allows you to scroll through the status of each metric. The control increases somewhat with the companion application, either on a smart phone or computer, to allow marginal additional flexibility. For instance, you might be able to provide profile information that calculates your stride, which is used to calculate the miles based on feet per step. You might be able to control whether you see your daily distance in miles or kilometers. These are limited systems, and the control you can exert over them is generally going to be limited as well.

Lack of control for a given device might not be a key limitation. As the world of the Internet of Things evolves, it is unclear how much this will change at the device level. Consumer devices will likely remain limited in what can be controlled. This isn't all bad, depending on the nature of the device. One could argue a smart phone is a form of an IoT-connected device. The control capabilities on a smart phone today are almost always greater than what the average user exploits or even understands. A connected car will have a similar level of configurability, and in many ways, be much like a smart phone itself. A smart toaster will be very limited, and with good reason.

Generally, the simpler, more singularly focused the IoT-enabled device, the more limited the user control will be at the device level. What's at issue, and what will surely change and evolve over time, is what happens at the application level.

For instance, what kind of control evolves for the person

looking at the fitness tracking application on their phone or computer will change, and it will do so in two ways. First, it will change as a function of the depth of control for the application consuming the sensor data. In other words, you'll be able to do more with your tracking application than you could before. You might be able to analyze the steps you take over a given month and note that you tend to go farther on Wednesday and the weekends, so you might try to figure out why and adjust to walk more on Monday and Tuesdays and Thursdays and Fridays. Perhaps it will give you the control to look at the data on an hourly basis, whereby you gain insight to your daily routine you did not have previously. These are very basic examples of extending the associated application and directly linked to the sensor data.

The big step comes in the control gained when the application in question is one of many. The implication here is that the sensor data is no longer directly (or exclusively) tied to the original consuming application, but now published into that application and others, or perhaps published into the direct consuming application but then republished out of that application into others. Likewise, the consuming application may be subscribing to other applications and consuming information from them, which taken in context with the fitness sensor data, may be much more informative. For instance, if the tracking data can be analyzed alongside vital sign information like heart rate and blood pressure, additional insight can be gained about how your body is responding to certain activities. The control of how this takes place has been largely limited to date, but is fact evolving in part based on demands in the market, and in part because organizations are recognizing the value of the data and the cost and ease of delivering against those market demands are getting easier and easier.

Can't leverage the data

Probably the most limiting factor of early systems has been the inability to leverage the underlying data. This is true across most of

IoT, where the device provider dictates the ownership and control of the data generated by the IoT device. Considering the possibilities of the data, the limitations associated with the inability to control the use of the data is significant. But as we alluded to above, this is changing. The change is happening in a variety of ways as well, but it is change nonetheless.

Let's go back to the example of the fitness tracker. In these cases, the exchange of data is happening on a peer-to-peer basis. This is no real standardized, normalized data model that is absorbing and enriching this fitness data. There are many applications out there, some tied to IoT-enabled devices, others simply existing as health and fitness applications, where the data is manually inputted or imported from other applications. If you look at the control capabilities of Apple Health, you'll see the SOURCES selection on the menu. This displays linked applications or devices that provide data into, or read data from Apple Health. These might be applications like MapMyRun, or MyFitnessPal, or Stretching or devices like and iPhone, Apple Watch, or Fitbit.

There are a growing number of sensor-enabled devices that are creating data, and a growing number of applications that are consuming data. While the early days of IoT was largely defined by IoT-enabled products—and the creation and the consumption of the data were self-contained into one delivery system—that world is changing. There is growing recognition that the value of the data created is increased, sometimes dramatically, by providing the data to a variety of consuming applications.

For instance, the number of miles you bike on a given day might be used by your cycling application to track your training. In your original cycling application that was tied to your on-bike "computer," that was exactly what happened. No more and no less. Now that same information is captured by an application resident on your smart phone that uses the phone's GPS to record your distance, speed (including split times), the course, as well as the elevation, and even the songs you listened to during the ride and the associated location and speed during each given song. A big improvement? Perhaps, but that is just the beginning.

This same data can be published into your more holistic fitness and nutrition application, which may be gathering your heart rate and blood pressure through other means, as well as your nutritional information based on the meals that were logged in your nutrition logger, determining how far above or below your caloric intake is and should be for you to maintain (or get to) your target weight.

Moreover, that same data might also be consumed by a bike maintenance application to track the wear and tear on your bike, and advise you as to when you need to perform basic maintenance. The bike manufacturer, that tracks thousands and thousands of other bikers as well, might also provide a commercial application. By collecting information about bike usage patterns and maintenance information, they might be able to provide proactive or preventative maintenance, as well as utilize the data to design future, arguably better products.

IoT's early limitations were the control and leverage of data. Most recognize and understand this, and in some ways, it is an easier problem to solve. The key is to understand the limitations of more narrowly scoped architectures and the extreme value of delivery architecture more holistic in nature.

Chapter 5

The Basic Challenges of Security and Privacy

The market, while still somewhat in its infancy, has matured to a point where there's widespread consensus that IoT security is paramount. Privacy is a related and critical consideration. Depending on whom you speak with, the concerns around security and privacy for IoT range from "no big deal" to the key issues that must be addressed to avoid what could certainly be catastrophic consequences.

For IoT to truly be effective, these issues should be addressed to the satisfaction of the market at large. It stands to reason that two of the key issues that will slow down the maturity and success of IoT are security and privacy. These aren't issues of technology, these are organizational, structural, and human issues. They are process issues.

For example, who is really responsible for securing the Internet of Things? Is it the CIO, or perhaps the newly named CISO? If there is a chief information security officer, he or she is the person likely responsible. But even then, what may seem obvious isn't always the case. These likely cross an organization's internal boundaries, and external ones as well. For instance, when looking at smart streetlights, is the IoT project controlled by the CIO or the department of transportation? For that matter, it might be the energy department. And when you install gunshot detection systems in the smart light poles, do they belong to the smart lighting owner, or the public safety department? In this equation, who it is that is looking out for the security elements of the solution? When the solution involves a smart product that is controlled by the product vendor, such as a Smart HVAC unit in the parking attendant booth at the city lot, is the smart connectivity the responsibility of the city or the HVAC vendor?

This is complicated further when the technology standards of the IoT-enabled, vendor supplied product are out of sync with the city standards for the city IT infrastructure. If the IoT-enabled product, like the HVAC unit, isn't considered a part of the IT infrastructure (which, at this point, probably isn't), then the security and privacy aspects of that asset could easily be overlooked. It certainly would not be the first time something like that happened.

There is the question as to how much data and what specific data is being collected. While surely some people know this answer, most don't. Nothing in recent reports would suggest anything other than what people think is being collected is probably less than what is actually being done. We know there are phone records: who you called; who called you; from where; when and for how long. It probably includes things like what type of handset you use; where you were during the call; where the other party was during the call; the carrier and more. It probably then contributes to further analysis about the frequency of your calls with particular people; others who interact with the same people; where they are, etc.

The data is the fuel. And this is just handsets and cell phone calls. When the number of IoT-deployed assets dwarf the number of cell phones put there, what else is being collected and by whom?

The other path of questioning is who it is that is actually collecting data. Is it the Service Providers? The IoT-enabled device providers? The city? Your company?

And more than that, why are they collecting the data? What

is it about the data that has value in the eyes of those collecting it? There is certainly value in the analysis of the data, which is the stated goal. Having data about what happened in the past is one thing. Using that data to determine what will happen in the future is another. While one can question the sincerity of what's being communicated, it's plausible that information being gathered about phone calls, Internet usage, emails, and file transfers can be used to detect patterns of behavior and predict future behavior.

> *The challenge is that nobody knows what is secure enough. Everyone talks about it for IoT, but what is not clear is what constitutes the point of satisfaction. The most fundamental element undermining privacy is the security consideration. If this protection is violated, then you broke the bargain.*
>
> *— Mario Finocchiaro*
> Vice President, Business
> Development LogMein/Xively

To the extent that the NSA, or for that matter, any organization, is attempting to provide security and protection, the questions and considerations around security and privacy are hardly easy. They are complex issues that have as much to do with policy and structure as they do with underlying technology.

Security is a given, but it may be a myth

In late 2014 at an IoT conference in Boston, a panelist remarked that he thought, "… the whole IoT security thing is getting blown out of proportion." The idea that anyone remotely following IoT would downplay the importance of IoT security seemed to catch most off guard.

It is one thing to hack a bank account. Not a good thing, of course, but a single account getting hacked isn't a call for national attention. Infiltrating a power grid, or nuclear station, or traffic grid, or many other infrastructure facilities is. The stakes are so very high. And once this happens, even in a small way, the faith in IoT will suffer a huge setback and IoT progress will halt for a period until the security safeguards are better established and certainly better communicated to all. This is likely to happen, although it would be fantastic if the market were to mobilize to avoid such an instance. Either way, the market is sure to drive an increased emphasis on security, either through thoughtful preparation or painful experience.

In a market obsessed with the advances in technology, the required response isn't quite so straightforward. "IT security techniques will not work for IoT services, suggesting there is a lot of work to do to secure the IoT," this according to Dr. Ulf Lindqvist, Program Director of SRI International, speaking at the CSIT World Cyber Security Technology Research Summit 2016.[26] This is a technology issue, and it most certainly is an operational and structural issue as well. The definitions around where responsibility and corresponding authority lie are much more complex with the Internet of Things.

We all ask, what can be done to safeguard solutions in the Internet of Things? What risks are inherent to smart grids? Mobile health? Smart cities? Are we more or less vulnerable when the Internet of Things is a reality? What are the security issues for the average person?

This is a big deal, and will require a great deal of thought, planning, coordination, and action. The more we consider, the bigger these issues becomes. Far more people care about basic security on the Internet, as we know it today, because the vulnerabilities are well documented.

The Internet of Things is all about scale. We have all been hearing the estimates: 50 billion connected devices by 2020, and some think this is low by a long shot. We know the number of devices producing information will be large. Next think of the use cases. Smart cities. Smart traffic systems. Smart cars. Mobile health. Smart grids. All of this is completely compelling, and can certainly change life as we know it.

---

26 http://www.infosecurity-magazine.com/news/current-it-security-will-not-work/.

Advances in engineering and technology have always been a two-edged sword. With the power, comes the implications of what power can do. Be it a sub-machine gun, a rocket ship, a laser beam, or breakthrough communications technology, the ability to achieve a better quality of life or greater productivity comes with the requirement to safeguard against improper use of these advances. Certainly, the Internet itself, as we sit today, has spawned a tremendous industry around security, with estimates around $50 to $60 billion.

Dealing with this won't be easy, and requires a great deal of thought, planning, coordination, and action.

The early signs of the Internet of Things are all around us. The refrigerator with the screen. The smart thermostat. Your TV connected to the Internet. The smart meter the power company installed and the corresponding information you received about how to better understand and adapt your energy usage to lower your costs without compromising your lifestyle.

This is the tip of the iceberg. Do you think most people are stopping to ask the right questions? What operating system is behind the screen on the fridge? Where is the smart meter storing my data? Can someone hack into my TV, my refrigerator, or my thermostat? If so, does that then open a backdoor into my home network, my computer, and my critical and confidential information? And again, this is just the house example.

What about the smart traffic grid connected to the smart city infrastructure? Does the electric grid or the water supply become vulnerable? Can your smart car be hacked and controlled, either putting you in danger or exposing confidential information about you? Will the great advances in mobile health translate into your medical information being accessed by the wrong people for the wrong reasons? These are all vulnerabilities. The implications of these are all bad. These are all very real concerns with not so easy answers. They are greater in magnitude and more far-reaching than most would contemplate (unless you work for the DOD or the NSA).

Answers won't come easy. Most seem to agree that a set of standards that drive the adoption and implementation of the Internet of Things would be helpful. One such standard is IPv6. The addressability of the Internet is all but tapped out with IPv4, yet that standard is relatively secure in its own right. There are certainly going to be issues exposed with IPv6, but the ultra-widespread adoption sure to come will help solidify it.

Yet, there are many, many more considerations. Standards bodies and industry groups, like the W3C, will try to help drive these, but it is unclear if the resulting standards will be industry driven, or steered by large, private companies who see value in getting to a standard quicker. Surely there are examples where this has happened in other industries, like financial services.

The big industry that exists for Internet security is likely to get even bigger, and interest in this will certainly accelerate as adoption of IoT progresses.

As startups rush to get in on the wave, the desire to deliver sexy features and functionality quickly to gain market share may usurp the desire to deliver solid, secure, scalable, well-considered architectures. In a market-driven economy with lots of money at stake, this is to be expected. But it's unfortunate because while the value of the IoT should be immense and life changing, the associated responsibility is all the higher as a result.

Another worthwhile question is to ask if the IoT makes the world safer or less safe? It is easy to conclude both. Again, the NSA, CIA, or similar organizations around the world can make a case for making the world a safer place by understanding this information.

If you are in the business of protecting anyone or anything, the more you know about potential threats, the better job you can do avoid or prevent them. The world being more or less safe is directly related to who is gaining this information and what the motivation is behind it.

To say "knowledge is power" certainly applies in all directions. If a government, a company, or some other non-state sponsored group decides they want to do harm and understands how to access data and analyze that information, then aren't we less safe as a result?

It would be hard to argue otherwise. This points out the significant imperative in safeguarding data. Furthermore, this has historically been discussed in the context of phone records, emails, and file transfers, which moving forward, is arguably a small subset of the scope of data which will be generated, so take the threat and magnify it ... significantly.

Who else is doing this? Absent from any of the discussions regarding the revelations in 2014 about the NSA is the question of who else might be collecting and analyzing this type of data. The hacking of the DNC and the numerous allegations that Russian hackers were behind it has certainly elevated the discussion of cyber security.

Why would one assume it's solely the US government or any government doing this? The mega players, ranging from the large mobile network operators around the world to Facebook, Google, Apple, and others all clearly can amass huge amounts of this type of data.

Most people would be surprised by the amount of browsing and other online or mobile data that can be collected by almost anyone. Look at the hundreds of companies in the Adtech space that are doing online advertising, mobile advertising, online auctions, brand management, and a variety of other use cases all-consuming this data. Most are clearly motivated less by a desire to inflict harm or invade privacy and more by the desire to make money. Yet, data is data. In some countries it is governed more strictly than in others, but accessing and analyzing this type of data is hardly the exclusive domain of the NSA.

One real problem that marks the early days of IoT is the inability to strike the balance between new, compelling features and ensuring proper security. In the rush to bring out IoT-enabled products, there is hard evidence some of the most basic considerations, like authentication, has gone overlooked. The ramifications of this are so far reaching that security alone for IoT is becoming its own major industry. We will see this in spades as we progress. All serious IoT players will have security, as a principle component of anything they offer, and will continue to make a bigger and bigger deal about it.

To frame the boundaries correctly, the optimist considers the perfect world where IoT makes everything easier, better, and more productive. That is the promise of IoT, and there is plenty of evidence to suggest our wildest dreams may be possible.

Conversely, cynical observers of the market suggest IoT's security challenges will account for the demise of the planet. Quite a strong statement, of course, but think about it. We may build, inadvertently, a more vulnerable planet, where countless people whose lives are ripped apart by cybercrime are overshadowed by catastrophic terror caused by subversion of nuclear power plants and power grids, corruption of water supply, disruption of normal life in the world's largest cities, and total destabilization of the world's economy brought about by a widespread breach of the world's financial markets. Not quite an uplifting picture, right?

Most people are not that cynical, and don't expect this is going to be the real outcome of the Internet of Things, but as we have already explored, when contemplating systems on such a massive scale, security considerations are extremely important. Getting that one wrong is clearly not a good option. There is certainly growing appreciation of this, and as such, the proper effort is increasingly being made to ensure safeguards. But these will not be trivial hatches to batten down, and it will take time and money to ensure it's done right.

Another consideration about security for IoT is the reach from the IT infrastructure into the physical infrastructure. Hackers may hack a bank account and steal money. We'd likely all agree that's a bad thing. But IoT security breaches can reach into the physical assets. The obvious leap is to the nuclear plants being compromised or the electrical grid being shut down. These are real concerns, to be sure. But there are likely to be exponentially more soft targets that are vulnerable to hacking. And while privacy and security go hand in hand, and privacy is certainly a major consideration, in most organizations security of the data, and in fact, security of the physical assets of the organization, are generally a top priority.

Surveys like the Global Consumer Survey conducted by the Mobile Ecosystem Trade Forum (MEF)[27] in early 2016 showed most people are concerned about trusting security. And just like a general best practice for any business has been to establish a business continuance strategy, it is becoming clear that organizations (be they small private commercial firms, educational entities, or large government entities) need to have cyber resilience strategies.

There have been multiple examples exposing this vulnerability. Cars have been hacked where control has been taken over by the hacker.[28] It is a pretty safe bet the auto industry cannot successfully evolve to deliver highly connected cars, much less autonomous driving, if they are getting hacked. And the danger ranges from those intent on harm, like deliberately crashing the car, to those who want to game the system by broadcasting an electronic emergency signal that instructs everything from the onboard electronics of the other cars on the road to the street lighting on the roadside to signal to move aside, ostensibly for an ambulance or police car to get by.

The twenty-one-year-old programming whiz wanting to make it to the Sharks' opening face-off game, however understandable to diehard hockey fans, isn't an acceptable example of the advances in our system. But these threats are far, far more pervasive than that.

Consider a light bulb. James Lyne, Head of Security Research at security software firm Sophos, tells the story of buying an

27 http://www.cio.com/article/3046688/security/searching-for-a-path-to-iot-security.html.
28 https://www.wired.com/2016/08/jeep-hackers-return-high-speed-steering-acceleration-hacks/.

inexpensive programmable light bulb and programming it to turn on and off 200 times per second. The outcome, as you might imagine, is an explosion followed by fire. There was virtually no authentication, and it was fairly easy for anyone with beginner skills to accomplish this. And while this might seem benign, it isn't. James conducted this experiment in his hotel room and set the hotel alarms off with one bulb.

This particular example shows both the ease in which IoT products introduced without the proper basic security can be manipulated. One can contemplate how easy it would be to use very low grade, seemingly harmless physical assets to create significant damage. What if every light bulb in a 500-room hotel is programmed to simultaneously explode at the same time? Now you have a hotel on fire. This isn't an easy thing.

The imperative exists, if not starts, with the companies producing IoT-enabled products. This brings us back to the trade-offs companies make when bringing these products to market. Right now, there is evidence that the opportunity to make money, as well as save money, and certainly to get the product to market faster is what guides the roadmap. If there is strong perceived benefit of an earlier, more feature-rich product introduction, and little to no perceived downside associated with the uncertainty of the security of the product, then the roadmap favors speed and functionality. This will not change until companies believe there is significant risk to the company, mainly in monetary terms, for not doing a better job in securing its offerings. This can come in the form of increased risk due to liabilities and subsequent potential monetary damages directly associated with the negative outcomes caused by lack of security. It can also come from the loss in brand equity of the product and the company at large resulting from the security issues.

The brand issue is a little trickier, because it is slower to develop, and likely will be interpreted differently by different constituents. At issue is where exactly the responsibility of a given companies lies in the delivering secure IoT products. If the consumers of those companies' products, or even those who aren't consumers but are somehow negatively impacted by those products begin to hold companies accountable for the ramifications of inadequate security, the needle will surely begin to move. This will cause the product companies to place a greater emphasis on security. We are already seeing this. The question is whether companies, and all organizations across all industries including government, will increasingly perceive this threat as being significant enough to be proactive in their efforts to avoid the issues before they become disastrous.

There is evidence to suggest this is happening on a broader basis now. Whether it's a topic of discussion at CISO gatherings or blogged about on sites like CHEIFIoT, contemplating organizational imperatives to secure IoT is growing. There is more being brought forward about proper checks and balances with IoT products, as well as IoT deployments. Companies are beginning to review their established security policies in the context of IoT, and update those policies accordingly. And since IoT crosses the IT and operational lines, organizations are beginning to address ownership and responsibility for these systems, inclusive of the security considerations.

The industrial sector, which has been the fastest mover, and arguably the greatest beneficiary of IoT to date, provides some good examples of the progress.[29] The stakes are high in this sector. The ramifications of a chemical plant shutdown or the hacking of a shipping port and subsequent disruption of operations poses a high risk to many. These instances are not only the potential target of those seeking monetary gain from theft, but also targets for misdeeds on much greater levels, including state-sponsored and non-state-sponsored terrorism.

This is becoming more understood by the day. As such, efforts to safeguard these systems have also evolved. There is growing recognition that rational approaches to network

29 http://www.zdnet.com/article/power-stations-trains-and-automobiles-protecting-the-industrial-internet-of-things/.

segmentation and other traditional strategies aren't enough for IoT-based deployments, where the scale of the contributing devices can go well beyond the traditional captive networks in both number and geographical reach. There are government and industry organizations encouraging best practices. The US Industrial Control Systems Cyber Emergency Response Team (US ICS-CERT) explains, "Organizations should isolate ICS networks from any untrusted networks, especially the Internet. All unused ports should be locked down and all unused services turned off ... Organizations should also limit remote access functionality wherever possible. Modems are especially insecure."

This only makes sense. The industrial control systems should not be subjected to access points that include workstations where an unknowing intern might open malware email or other social network launched attacks. That doesn't mean that there isn't still external vulnerability. Many IoT systems, including industrial ones, reach outside the isolated networks of the organization, where sensors might be deployed in remote devices in homes, on infrastructure, or other devices that carry with them certain vulnerabilities.

The response to security is a growing push towards best practices. These vary from group to group. We don't often see consulting firm A espousing the same best practices as consulting firm B. That said, there is growing consensus around minimal best practices for drastically reducing, if not avoiding the likelihood of hacking. These include but aren't limited to:

- Designing your network and deployment architecture with the ability to update them as needed.
- Look to open systems. Despite how that might seem, the open standards will tend to be more secure, so stay away from closed, proprietary systems.
- Stay away from "backdoors." Apple is probably a good one to speak to about this.
- Use private keys inside devices, and make sure you keep those keys private.

- Ensure the basics are done correctly—like the use of passwords and authentication techniques. With third party devices, these should never be assumed to be adequate without a complete understanding of the security characteristics of the device and how that device interactions with your deployment architecture.
- Employ monitoring techniques and tools to ensure the ongoing safety of the network, while enhancing your ability to respond quickly when something does appear questionable.
- There are a variety of opinions about the use of public clouds. At the most basic level, this may add concerns, especially depending on whether the applications themselves are running in the cloud, or if just the data is being stored there. This isn't to suggest the cloud is bad, per se, but rather an important consideration that should be understood and contemplated in the overall deployment architecture.

There are a myriad of published best IoT practices available online. An example of another view comes from the Federal Trade Commission, where they identify five basic business principles:

- Take stock. Know what personal information you have in your files and on your computers.
- Scale down. Keep only what you need for your business.
- Lock it. Protect the information you keep.
- Pitch it. Properly dispose of what you no longer need.
- Plan ahead. Create a plan to respond to security incidents.

Security will continue to evolve as the market matures.[30] As it does, now technologies will accompany security contemplations, ranging from biometric scanning to the use of distributed ledgers (known as "blockchain"). The architectures and the means of protecting IoT will increase in sophistication, as will the capabilities of the hackers.

Threats won't stay the same, but evolve along with the

---

30 https://www.cisecurity.org/controls/

technology. Hopefully we won't find the market dramatically influenced by horrific events and that gaps that are exploited, but rather, steadily evolve in a manner that plans and provides the right levels of protection to avoid such events. To the extent companies take it upon themselves to do this that would be great. We all understand that while only some will, others, for a variety of reasons but mostly to drive revenue and curtail expenses, will not. There will most certainly be consequences as result.

In some instances, we will see an increasing push from government regulation. Not unlike the issues and excesses of the financial markets, sometimes the regulatory environments are established to provide a commonsense safety net to protect the well-being of all, based on the potential miscalculations, though often based on increased wealth/revenue of a few. This always comes with loud objections from those that are inhibited, in some form or fashion, from what they would do otherwise, but that is somewhat the point.

The idea around most regulations is less often the line created by the regulation itself, but rather where that line is drawn. IoT security is clearly an area where there will likely be regulatory oversight. Market demands will hopefully evolve to greater recognize the importance of security, and even further, that companies take such initiatives ahead of regulatory mandate. We shall see.

Privacy may not be a given, nor is it obvious

Privacy is another material consideration that can hold back the adoption of IoT on a widespread basis. This will become more of an issue once people begin to appreciate how privacy works in the context of how IoT could be compromised.

When the City of Chicago in concert with Argonne National Labs and others began to rollout the "Array of Things" project, people began to believe that the technology was capable of tracking their movements through the city. The idea of Big Brother watching didn't go over well, and a slight uproar ensued, causing the city to ensure the proper communication was in place before proceeding. Not further technological accommodation, per se, but communication. This highlights a key point. The city was never planning to make personal information about anyone available to anyone, including to the city itself. It had taken steps to sterilize information as a part of the project. But that wasn't communicated as clearly, as it should have been, so people jumped to the conclusion that the citizens would be compromised relative to privacy. This is what undermines trust, and trust is a critical element in IoT's success.

> *Privacy is a value to be negotiated with a vendor. People will exchange privacy for value. The margin between the brand and the customer is the value they get for the privacy they relinquish.*
> — *Mario Finocchiaro*
> *Vice President, Business Development LogMein/Xively*

Since the technology is certainly capable of exposing a great deal of personal information about you, from your energy usage to your daily routines to your driving habits, the mechanisms for accommodating this must be both put in place, and very clearly communicated so the average person understands and trusts how the IoT systems will treat their privacy. When it comes to any IoT system, one of the key elements of deploying these systems should be complete transparency about what is being collected and why. This will build trust and confidence in these systems and go a long way to ensure their adoption and success.

For now, of course, for the Internet of Things, a secure planet doesn't necessarily equate to a private one. Your house may be secure, but it might still be made of glass. The governance issues may be the toughest to address. Who owns data? Who administers data? Who determines how data standards are set, how data is organized, how it is kept, where it is kept, as well as who can see it and use it and for what purposes?

The security issues may be huge, but there should be large-scale agreement regarding the security goals and thus gaining agreement on addressing those challenges should ostensibly be easier to come by. Not so much for governance. The subtle (or not so subtle) byproduct of this consideration is economic opportunity, or lack thereof, of certain organizations, companies, classes of companies, or governments along the way.

What happens if Apple or Google or Microsoft sets the bulk of the standards? Just kidding, of course. Or am I? How many people worried about Microsoft, Apple, or Google having undue influence based on the data they have? Moreover, how many people had heard of Facebook twelve years ago, and now, how many people worry about its ability to use and manipulate data?

Once you have had the change to seriously interact with people from Facebook, Apple, Google, and Microsoft, you might be, perhaps naively, less worried about how personal data will be manipulated as it relates to individuals. The idea behind most analysis and corresponding action based on this data is to make the individuals' lives better. That's how money gets made. The bigger question is where is the money getting made, how, and why? These issues are thorny. They take time to address. And they will likely be resolved through a much more iterative process, perhaps with a fair amount of difficulty along the way.

It is worth considering what data can and might be collected in the future, and the trade-offs associated with this data. This is where it gets really, early interesting. If you are spooked by call data records, then what about your energy usage, or your driving habits, or your walking habits and whereabouts, or your buying habits, eating habits, whatever?

One of the compelling aspects of the Internet of Things is that the world can become somewhat tailored and much more efficient to you, as an individual, because data can be understood and interpreted in the context of what makes your life better, from energy management to transportation to shopping and more. But for this to work, the data must be there, and in the hands of people or organizations with the malicious intentions, it can certainly pose an increasingly large problem.

Many of the organizations, which have contended with the privacy issues for some time, have developed strategies for privacy. This may include the stewardship of data, where you control the data about you. This may be a bit misleading, in that you might designate who sees your posts on Facebook, but not necessarily how your underlying habits or contributed content are interpreted and used, even when anonymized.

There are strategies being deployed that take staged authentication, where the data available at the lowest level (think the "edge device") are segmented from upstream stages, where the data available to the successive tiers become more aggregated, filtered, and anonymized.[31] This is where authentication is extremely important. The authentication of IoT devices will be different, in many ways, than the authentication of laptops or smart phones. In the latter, we are seeing increased use of biometric authentication, like fingerprint recognition. We are also seeing two-phase authentication, which is especially prevalent in companies that depend on trust, but have suffered high profile hacks like Yahoo and Dropbox.

Privacy concerns with IoT extend fairly far and wide. One noteworthy aspects of IoT is the ability to integrate with cameras and microphones for surveillance.

With the size and cost of video technology dropping and the quality increasing, the number of cameras deployed in conjunction with IoT is increasing dramatically (recall the three cameras in the Samsung refrigerator). But this also presents concerns associated with both outright hacking into video feeds as well as the non-hacked, but potentially improper use of those feeds. For instance, can the smart TV providers access cameras and microphones on your TV? Can BMW or Audi access the feeds from the multiple onboard cameras in your car? What are the limitations of this? How far will this technology extend, and to what extent will people's privacy potentially be compromised?

---

31 http://www.information-age.com/privacy-and-authenticatio n-internet-things-123461082/.

It turns out, people seem to care quite a bit about this. In smart city efforts, there have certainly been civic outcries to challenge, and in many ways, simply better understand what exactly is being collected and how that information is used. Whether it's video feed or power meter data or beacon data or anything else, people want to understand how much of their habits, preferences, and actions—their very lives—are being revealed. Overlooking privacy issues will kill certain IoT initiatives. It is a big deal, and organizations and product companies should all care deeply about this topic. To the extent organizations can address these issues upfront and head-on, the chances of acceptance of associated IoT deployments will increase.

I see the top 2 concerns for smart homes being security and privacy. Some people speak with want to understand, when speaking about the data, where does their ownership and privacy begin and end? What pieces of the data being collected belong to them and what pieces belong to the apartment or office building? At the same time, we now live in a culture when asking about use Facebook, everyone still uses, but all seemed concerned about privacy.
— Chad Curry
Managing Director at National Association of REALTORS

The Battle Lines: Who owns the Data?

When it comes to the Internet of Things, we should ask how and whether markets—and too human life—might flourish, as well as the concentration and distribution of the associative powers and resources. Just as there are ethical and geopolitical issues associated with natural resource utilization, as data becomes, in a very real sense, a natural resource, there will be moral considerations, ones that cross international borders as well as social norms. Controlling data is similar to controlling oil reserve or farmland or water access. Will control fall to the more powerful government or perhaps a confederacy of governments? Or will mega-corporations control these spheres of influence? Consider the "democratization of data." Should data be made accessible? And to whom? And for what purpose or purposes? If, as some say, "data is the new oil," there will be posturing, strong-arming, and certain power struggles around how data is controlled, utilized, and who the main beneficiaries will be.

Will IoT enhance the quality of life for all people, or a fraction of the population? This is basically the next obvious question beyond the discussion above. One could ask if all mankind benefits from more efficient energy delivery, or if all people enjoy longer lives due to increased mobile health capabilities. Will the average person gain quality time in their days due to smart cars and more efficient traffic grids? They should. But then again, many would argue poverty rates and the number of indigent people shouldn't be near what they are in some of the wealthiest countries in the world. It will be interesting to watch how the Internet of Things is realized and how it unfolds. One can only hope IoT's beneficiaries run far and wide. In fact, in some ways, those who benefit the most could well be those in the world who have the least now. As energy delivery, healthcare delivery, and food production improve, one could argue that this should lead to a better world. But if data really is the new oil, then the market will need to grapple with how and why data ownership and stewardship evolves, and this will not be easy.

Why capital equipment vendors own the data

While it might be easy to take aim at capital equipment providers for the stance on ownership and control that has largely been taken about the data, if you step back it is understandable. They're the ones who introduce the IoT-enabled devices. Whether it is Fitbit or Withings or Lutron or Sub-Zero on the consumer side, or Bosch or Johnson Controls or Honeywell or John Deere on the commercial side, the delivery of smart equipment and devices, including the messages being generated and consumed, are a part of these offerings. At the onset, they were almost all self-contained, closed-loop, message-response systems. Messages are generated and fed into a workflow or rules engine, which interprets the message to determine if a threshold has been crossed and any alert or action needs to be taken. The buyers of these offerings (or at least, the majority of them) were likely not thinking about how they, as individuals, would use the data itself, but rather how compelling it was that they were alerted when the refrigerator door was left open, or how they could control the lights from their iPhone, or how exhilarating it was to see "You've walked 22,318 steps today. Nice job, Betty! A new personal best." The ownership of the data was hardly in question at first.

Then, as the capital equipment vendors began to appreciate the value of this data a little more, the idea of using this for predictive maintenance became the obvious next step. This makes sense, of course, and is hardly a new idea. Sensor messages from capital equipment have been around for a long time, where the data was used for predictive maintenance. In 1991, Hitachi Data Systems had a system called "HiTrack," which captured all the logs from the disk drives they had in the field. HiTrack was a predictive maintenance application the analyzed the logs and alerted local field support if a drive was trending towards a crash. They, in turn, would schedule a planned maintenance visit to replace the soon to be faulty drive. This is basically what the predictive maintenance applications associated with IoT-enabled devices are doing today. The sensors are more advanced, and the communications are via Internet and IPv6 addressability, instead of a disk drive that quite literally phones home. Even so the data and the desired outcomes are very similar. At the time, Hitachi's customers were somewhat in awe of this capability, and there was little evidence of customers arguing that they needed ownership and control of the data. While some probably did, most were simply appreciative of the capability. This appreciation bred loyalty and recurring revenues, which is key to the equation.

For these reasons, it isn't surprising that the capital equipment vendors want to own (and control) data. In fact, part of the argument is that they, and only they, know best what to do with the data. This is probably true, and their point is a valid one, but only to a degree. If a company makes an industrial lighting system, they should, by all rights, have deep expertise in lighting systems, certainly, more than the companies that

All the barriers to entry have come down – silicon, cloud, data. A lot of people are starting to think the value of IoT is in the data. And when you put the customer at the center, the expectations are going up.

— Mario Finocchiaro
Vice President, Business Development LogMein/Xively

purchase and install them. And if the lighting company has a population of 6000 customers who have installed their lighting systems, then it stands to reason that gathering operational information about the entirety of that population will yield insight into, among other actionable directives, predictive maintenance. For example, the information may show that customers in warm and humid factories tend to burn out faster than ones in better temperature controlled retail environments, leading to design changes to provide better insulation for a newly created factory version. Such data is also useful in understanding customer behavior, and to provide increased servicing as well. Predictive maintenance eliminates unnecessary downtime and outages caused by failing equipment, but there are other servicing benefits as well. A service engineer working with the customer's exact data would likely be able to troubleshoot issues in ways that never existed before such data was available. This creates a much better experience for the customer, and again, increases the loyalty and stickiness of the relationship.

Then there is the argument around firmware—which is different from the data argument, but serves to re-enforce the thesis of the capital equipment vendor retaining ownership and control. The firmware argument is that the equipment that they provide contains firmware that needs to be updated on an ongoing basis. Not unlike your iPhone or Galaxy, IoT-enabled equipment is being constantly upgraded and debugged. Hopefully, this increases performance, functionality, and security. This is done via firmware in the device or device header, which is managed remotely by the equipment vendor. Their argument here is their duty, versus their customer's duty, to manage their firmware Again, this is a valid argument. In fact, you should want the vendor to be able to do this. You have become accustomed to this with apps on your phone and on your computer, but may not realize that your AppleTV, your Next Thermostat, and your Ford are all doing the same thing. Cars have had firmware in them for quite some time. Firmware is typically updated when the car is serviced, and the idea is nothing new. Such ongoing updating helps users, and it helps the product supplier, regardless of the product.

There is a counterargument, both to the ownership of the data and the management of the firmware. The vendor can still get exactly the same data they were getting before without having to own it, and they can control the firmware, as well, with little or no change to the process. Copying and propagating data has a near zero cost associated with it. There is nothing hard about the owner of an IoT subsystem ingesting the data and still sending the same data on to the equipment provider. In fact, you want that. Why? Because as we discussed above, nobody knows their equipment like they do, as they will say, and you want the benefit of that insight. As far as firmware goes, that capability can easily be added to the *first receiver* of the data, which is either a physical or virtual server, much like a printer driver allows an equipment provider to continue to maintain the system via the firmware.

Equipment vendors won't easily concede to this. This is because when they own the data, they can control what is done with the data, how it is seen, and how it is used. For example, you may be able to see some data from your connected HVAC, but you probably cannot download the entirety of the data collected and create your own dashboards or run your own analytics. It's worth asking, who the "you" is in this example? A person, a city, a company? As you the person, you the city, or you the company invest in more and more IoT subsystems, the leverage and insight one gains from the introspection of that data, especially in the context of other IoT subsystem data, will provide insight one would logically never otherwise get. For instance, if you are running an industrial distribution site, you might have door sensors at multiple docks, sensors in the lighting, sensors in the HVAC, sensors for humidity, sensors for certain gases, sensors on the forklifts, and many other areas as well. If you can gather the data from all the IoT-enabled products, from the forklifts to the cargo doors to the lighting system and more, you may be able look at the IoT data from one subsystem in the context of the others. You might be able to see a correlation between the lighting levels and forklift driver productivity. You might see a correlation between the temperature and the dock door status. These are easy examples, but over time, the complexity of these systems and the data available will become much, much greater. At that point, the richness of the signature that can be derived from the data increases dramatically, as does the corresponding insight, but you must be able to use that data to achieve that benefit.

For most product providers today, controlling data is a part of controlling the overall experience, which ties back to the loyalty and stickiness of the relationship. If the owner of the subsystem gets the data, they might start writing their own applications, or there might even be a cottage industry of third party applications riding on top of the *first receiver* or at other constituencies in the ecosystem that could undermine the more exclusive initial relationship. It is in the product provider's best interests to control the data, but it isn't necessarily in the best interests of the product owner, in most cases, that being the enterprise. The key to this equation, especially since the enterprise will benefit by having the product owner get the data and to be able to control the firmware, is that you want them to be able to get this, just not at your expense. It does not need to be an either/or decision. To the extent that data is directly ingested by the owner of the product, then propagated to the product vendor, ostensibly along with certain contractual obligations governing that flow of data, then, to an extent, both can win. While this may be a less desirable option for product providers, if and when the market shifts to demand these capabilities, it will become table stakes for product providers, and to remain competitive, they'd need to agree to such a model where the owner of the product maintains control of the data in the context of certain contractual obligations protecting the product provider.

Delineating ownership, stewardship, and access

It may be compelling to have all this new IoT-enabled equipment in your home or business, but as we discussed above, at some point organizations will come to grips with the fact that if they could use all that data, as opposed to simply being relegated to how it's provided via the product supplier, then they could do so much more with it. With this realization comes a push to either own the data, or at least have access to all the data from these systems. People and organizations are beginning to recognize this and demand ownership of the data.

This concept is somewhat nuanced. An owner of data isn't necessarily the steward of the data. Data stewardship refers to the care and at least partial control over how the data is used, and by whom. Think of this as how Facebook controls who can see your posts. In an IoT world, if the de facto owner of the data becomes the enterprise or organization that has purchased and is using the various IoT subsystems, then one might assume that data stewardship rests with the same party. In many cases this would be true. But there are certainly variations on this theme.

A fast food restaurant might have smart HVAC, several units of smart kitchen equipment, smart lighting, a beacon system, smart thermostats, an IoT-enabled security system and an IoT-enabled entertainment system. It would make sense that the person managing this site also controls the data. But what does that mean? For starters, this means they would want to take all the data coming from the various equipment and persisted it into a common model. Either while the incoming data is in flight, or once persisted into the database, they could perform certain computational analytics against the data. They could filter out the inconsequential messages, like temperature readings that stay the same for long periods of time. They could perform aggregation of the data. They could compute basic statistics coming from the data. But the interesting part would be how that data is then consumed and by whom.

One of the obvious consumers of that data would be the local restaurant itself. That data could form the basis of an optimization system that links the granular signature coming off the various IoT data with the local point-of-sale system, inventory system, and crew-scheduling system. They may even enrich the database with other local information such as pedestrian traffic, street traffic, and weather data. They may also want to publish this data to an analytic workbench to monitor operational analytics to better understand what's going on at any particular time. Investigative analytics can provide an analysis of why something is happening, and predictive analytics help create a richer understanding of what will be happening, whether in regards to the physical assets themselves, or more importantly, to the owner of the operation. In fact, this also lends itself to the creation of machine learning algorithms, where the IoT systems become adaptive in nature, and the optimization required is self-tuning. Ostensibly this would all be geared to optimizing revenue and minimizing expenses.

Other consumers of this data might be the restaurant chain's regional or corporate office. It's unlikely these entities want to see the same level of granularity as the local consuming applications. They are more apt to look for certain aggregate, computed information coming from the main immediate repository, which again, we are calling the *first receiver*. If the restaurant itself is a franchised restaurant, it is quite possible that the owner of the data might be the franchisee, while the steward of the data might well be the corporate entity.

Another key consumer of this data is the product manufacturer. While previously, in most IOT systems, the product providers would be delivering the IOT-enabled products and directly consuming the data coming from those products, the *first receiver* architecture will expect product providers to create agreements with the user of their products, in this case, the restaurant owner or operator, in order to receive the data they need. It is highly likely that these will exist as contractual agreements that are a function of purchasing the product in first place

There are certainly other potential consumers of this data as well. Third party supply chain partners and regulatory oversight bodies are two likely candidates. They may prescribe how they need certain data, but it would be left up to the owner of that data to work with the various entities to ensure the right data is delivered in the right way at the right time. In this regard, the consumers of this data are looking for access to the data, but that access would likely be limited to read only, and the access will also likely be limited from a security and privacy standpoint as well.

Now let's look at another example, a smart city. A smart city project may have several elements in it ranging from smart energy to smart parking to smart lighting to enhanced policy and security systems and many, many more. The question as to how this all comes together, and at a more granular level, how the human and technological efforts plays out, isn't an easy and straightforward effort. This all ultimately speaks to the issues and drivers behind who owns the data, who controls the data, and who has access to the data.

> *With the Array of Things deployed on a widespread basis, we will have the opportunity to create in one place the most comprehensive database about cities, allowing measurement in a consistent, uniform way. So for example, a local government wants to contract a new park. This would let them better understand how it would affect the neighborhood. It will enable people to do policy and science research and gain a better understanding about the cities. By using the aggregated database, researchers and planners can leverage the network effect of the data. A big part of the appeal is that this is being provided as open source, open data and not through a huge company with proprietary ownership and control over the data.*
> *— Charlie Catlett*
> *Director, Urban Center for Computation and Data (urbanCCD)*

The taxpayers fundamentally fund systems procured by the city. In theory, the citizens of the city paid for the systems, and therefore the case can be made that they should also own the data, but again, ownership and control can easily become tricky topics. A city might put several smart systems out to bid. These could include smart lighting, smart parking, smart surveillance, and a gunshot detection system. Ultimately, tax-paying citizens foot the bill, but at an operational level, departmental budgets are funding these. But which department should it be? Is the IT Department? It might be, but it also might be the Streets and Sanitation Department. Lighting could also fall under streets but could well be transportation or energy. The surveillance system could be either of those, but more likely it's the police and public safety department, who are likely candidates for the gunshot system, except for the fact that the gunshot system might actually be installed in the light poles of the smart lighting system, so this too becomes less clear.

Then there's data sharing. Regardless of the departmental "owner," who can see the data and use the data? Who determines these answers? This has many repercussions. Let's begin with some basic elements, the sharing of data amongst departments. A couple of easy examples are that the gunshot detection needs to work in conjunction with the surveillance system, as well the smart lighting system.

If a gunshot is detected, the cameras need to immediately repoint to the location of the shot. Moreover, the smart lighting system should brighten the area. This requires that the data be shared. There is a basic expectation of systems integration. Another example might be the dispatching of emergency vehicles. These vehicles will need to broadcast messages that integrate with traffic flow to open lanes and crossroads, as well as broadcast messages to cars on the road via known blinking patterns or color changes to let people know of an incident underway, or more likely, to broadcast that same signal to be consumed by autonomous cars so they can respond accordingly. The point is, these systems cannot operate in isolation or the city fails to be "smart."

Then there is the external view, meaning, who else can "see" and use the data, and who can benefit (monetarily) from the data? There are more and more cities moving to the idea of an open data environment for smart cities, meaning, they publish the data they collect. But even this is within certain tolerances. If they are collecting loads of data like what is being done in the Array of Things project in Chicago, then the idea is that the information collected is available to everyone in real time.

There are some instances where vendors provide improved services via specific smart city offerings, but then own and control the data and thus, can monetize that data themselves. There are other instances where the vendors are working with the city to further monetize the data for the benefit of the city, but the data itself is distributed, at least in part, as a value added, fee-based service.

There are two key takeaway points when looking at a smart city. First, the concept of ownership and governance can be complex on both a technological and human level, and second, the deployment architecture must allow for the data being consumed from various systems to be utilized in the context of other systems, so separating the creation of the data from the consumption of the data is critical.

It's really about control and the nuances of this.

The debate about ownership is a debate about control. With this in mind, the best strategy to navigate such a debate is to view the situation through each constituent's lens. The two most critical constituents are the IoT enabled product suppliers, and the Enterprises that purchase and use these IoT-enabled products. Other constituents like supply chain partners and regulatory oversight groups logically fall into the category of those being granted access to the data, but they're almost never in a position to own or fundamentally control the data. They're more apt to consume the data in a way that allows them to re-purpose it for other specific uses.

Revisiting the view of the IoT enabled product supplier, there are clear and obvious reasons why they would want to own and control the data. Their clear goal is to make money. They do this by having customers buy their products, which happens because they provide products the customers like. By better larverging the data from these IOT-enabled products, they can enhance the product quality and service offerings which contribute to these goals.

IoT-enabled products can do all that. If a company provides a smart HVAC unit,

> *Today, there is a sense that the creator or owner of the asset owns the data. But owning is less important in the equation. People and organizations more concerned about continuing to provide value, so control of the data is more important than actual ownership. Product providers are being more transparent as to what they plan to do with the data.*
>
> *— Matt Jennings*
> *Regional President, Americas Bosch Software Innovations*

they can make controlling that unit easy for the customer. They can do predictive maintenance on the unit to offset problems and downtime that might otherwise undermine the relationship. And if there's a problem, the IoT-enabled nature of the product can allow the service center to quickly diagnose issues up to and including "looking at the unit" via a smart phone's camera app that remotely enables a service technician to be in front of the unit. All of this creates brand loyalty to these relationships that suppliers want. It's also good business. Why wouldn't the customer want this too?

The simple answer is that they do. If data from the HVAC unit is owned and controlled by the supplier, then the enterprise cannot leverage that data in the context of other data they're creating and using. For instance, they may have a smart energy system, complete with smart thermostat, fans, window blinds, floor heating and other systems that could be optimized, provided all systems could produce data that could be analyzed in the context of one another. In doing so, a more granular signature is being created and, based on insights gained from the data, all participating systems could then be coordinated and optimized. But if the HVAC, or any of the systems in question, ties the creation of the data exclusively to the consumption of that data, then you take away the ability to perform the holistic analysis and take the appropriate action.

This isn't to say the enterprise doesn't want the supplier doing all the things they can do with their IOT-enabled systems. It most certainly does. It just doesn't have to be at the expense of the enterprise's ability to leverage the data more effectively. The difference here is that the relationship is inverted. The enterprise should want (or demand) to own the data, but then be willing to contractually agree to supply the vendor with either the exact same data stream they were already getting, or perhaps some enriched version of the stream that might prove even more beneficial to the product vendor. For instance, the vendor may get the HVAC stream only and do what they've always done.

But they may get a stream that includes additional information like the ambient temperature, the electrical load in the house or building, and humidity. In this regard, the product vendor could, in turn, gain additional insights that were previously unavailable. These are contractual and business issues (and opportunities). The thing the product vendor loses in this equation is maximum control, because the leverage shifts to the enterprise.

If a product vendor isn't providing the right level of product quality and service up to the predictive maintenance and high-end servicing capabilities, as described above, it becomes easier for buyers and system users to switch to a competitor. This creates a battleground, but once market momentum shifts to the point where enterprises demand ownership and control of the data (while recognizing the true symbiotic relationships they have with the vendors), delivering products that provide this capability to the enterprise buyer will become accepted market requirements.

Chapter 7

The Challenge of Governance

The issues associated with security and privacy will ultimately be inextricably tied to the governance associated with the IoT deployment of a given organization, or possibly, but usually not, the capital equipment provider or downstream recipient of your data. To understand this, it's important to look at general governance, governance in the context of IoT, and some of the drivers behind how this is evolving and why.

As IoT began to evolve from M2M, most early deployments were somewhat akin to M2M systems being deployed over the Internet. Specifically, most early IoT projects have been deployed as closed-loop, message-response systems. By 2016 we had begun to see changes to this, and these changes will continue to pick up momentum. The reason for this is the data. It will become increasingly clear the critical value for IoT is realized in the data, where the underlying data will be used by a variety of consuming applications.

However, to facilitate this, deployment architectures must contemplate how messages travel from ingestion to use in consuming applications, including the cleansing and enriching process, especially at the point of *first receiver*. As we previously discussed, this calls out the question of ownership and stewardship of the data, which in turn speaks to security and privacy issues.

To provide ideal leverage of IoT data for all consuming constituencies, these architectural and governance issues should be addressed. Those organizations that do this with well-considered deployment architectures will likely be big winners, and those that do not will likely suffer as a result. There's a growing amount of anecdotal evidence to suggest that more and more organizations want access to, if not outright ownership of the IoT data created by their deployed IoT subsystems, and this will increasingly force this issue.

The role of standards will become increasingly important. Lack of standards will prevent adoption on a broad scale. For the Internet of Things to work, there must be broad adoption. You can't have smart cars, smart cities, and widely-connected, well-functioning systems, if the parts don't fit together.

When Michael Porter and Jim Heppleman wrote about the progression from smart connected products to product systems to systems of systems, they foreshadowed a world where the linkages implied by "system of systems" becomes an imperative. If everyone's phone only worked with the exact same type of phone, phone systems would not work (well). If appliances all required different electrical plugs, that wouldn't work either. The examples are endless. Lug nuts on cars. Traffic lights. TV Signals. Keyboards (pianos and computers).

There are, of course, limitations. You have metric and imperial measurement systems. Some countries use NTSC video encoding, while others use PAL. Appliance standards only go so far. There are five major key variations of "standard" plugs depending on where you live. Getting a "connected world" or a "smarter planet" or "Industrial Internet" or "Internet of Everything" makes assumptions about certain standards that aren't likely to just fall into place.

Organizations like the W3C[32] are working hard to get there. There are other initiatives in Europe and Asia pushing standards as well. Clearly there are more than a few companies that would

---

32 http://www.w3.org

like to set de facto standards. The progress to allow for standards and interconnectivity will happen, but there will be many battles that continue to be fought along the way. Underpinning all of this is the consideration around governance for IoT and what that means for IoT efforts becoming effective.

What does governance mean for IoT?

The most basic explanation for governance of data is the framework that's established—ostensibly by the owner of that data—as to who can see and use the data and to what extent. This is usually the domain of the information technology department or division within a given organization.

For the Internet of Things, it's a little trickier, in part because the drivers of these systems are often operational and not the technology groups. So, defining where the responsibility for this lies in a given organization may be quite different from one organization to another. Add to this that the motivations of specific operational groups could easily be different from the drivers of the organization at the highest level, which ostensibly would be the view of IT (although many would argue that doesn't hold either).

In a Dataversity slide deck from 2015, data governance is defined as the "execution and enforcement of authority over the management of the data and data-related resources," and data stewardship as the "formalization of accountability over the management of data and data related resources." [33]

In a traditional enterprise (pre-IoT), this function largely sits in the IT organization, and makes decisions about a broad range of considerations about the data. This includes considerations about how and where the data is created, how the quality of the data is addressed, who has responsibility for the data, how privacy is managed, and how protection of the data is ensured. The data governance function of these enterprises establishes

---

33 http://www.slideshare.net/Dataversity/data-governance-and-the-Internet-of-things?

policies and procedures to address all this. This also extends to assessing elements such as risk management and compliance obligations.

Governance is a detailed and dynamic imperative for most enterprises. The classification system that might be adopted to classify and store the data today might need to adapt to changes in the environment tomorrow. The type of metadata that's collected and how that metadata is used is also a governance consideration. At the heart of the governance function, though, is making sure the right person or entity gets the right data at the right time in the right way.

Who can see, who can use, who cares?

The governance function needs to understand who the "right person or entity" is. What defines someone who should see all or some portion of data? This can be difficult in a traditional enterprise, but when you extend the data being created to thousands or millions of devices, the challenge increases dramatically. This can be a function of business relationships. This can be a function of contractual relationships. But access rights can be changed, so there needs to be clear delineation as to who can actually put those changes in motion, and under what (arguably strict) criteria.

And what is the "right data"? Again, this is subject to interpretation. Generally speaking, the "right data" considers the context of how the data is being consumed, so "what's right" for a remote location that also happens to be producing the data, like a fast-food restaurant, where the use is its point of contact and inventory systems and related dashboarding and alerting systems might be different than "what's right" for the corporate or regional hub operations. "What's right" for the various vendors, who have IoT subsystems running in the restaurant, is probably the same thing they'd have gathered, absent the restaurant capturing that data, as a first step locally. Although the vendor may benefit from the restaurant's ability to filter and cleanse the data as well, and, therefore, may refine their definition. FDA or supply chain partners requiring access to this data may have other definitions that suit their needs. The role of governance is to provide the framework for how the data gets classified internally, as well as how it gets propagated internally and externally.

In an ideal world, everyone would get what they want. The problem with this is that for entity A to get what they want, often comes at the expense of entity B getting what they want. This doesn't necessarily need to be the case with IoT. Perhaps the key driver for the *first receiver* model is to provide for all entities in the ecosystem to see maximum leverage from the IoT data. This is largely possible, in part, due to the (near) zero marginal cost of propagating data to multiple constituents. The main complicating factor stems from the provider of the IoT subsystems, who in many cases has contractual expectations of ownership and control of the data.

Because there are external third parties involved, the role of security becomes all the more critical, so this may require collaboration as well. Also important in this equation is the semantic interpretation of the data. The FDA may be looking for codes or nomenclature different from the governing entity, so while there is an ability to propagate raw atomic or cleaned and enriched data in a variety of different forms or subsets, there is also a need for a shared definition of exactly what the data actually means in order for it to be properly used.

At the heart of the *first receiver* concept is data primacy. Therefore, the role of governance becomes the central oversight in ensuring the environment is correctly maintained. This effects privacy in that governance rules dictate, down to the field of record, what data can be revealed to what party and under what condition.

Likewise, governance plays a key role in security, as the overall security model is informed by the very rules established within the governance framework, but those establishing the framework must clearly understand the reach of security imperatives and the

potential constraints that imposes on how the data can be social-
ized. In the end, the role of governance by the primary owner
of the data becomes the very important caretaker of viability of
the IoT operational architecture and the resulting leverage both
within and beyond the enterprise.

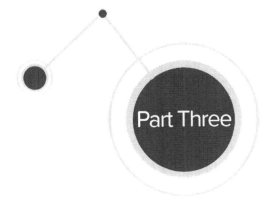

Part Three

Where We Are Headed: An Event-driven, Publish, and Subscribe Deployment Architecture

"Almost all quality improvement comes via simplification
of design, manufacturing ... layout, processes,
and procedures."
–Tom Peters

Chapter 8

The Utility Value of Data

Let's start with the basic systems. A closed-loop message response system, where a Coke machine is instrumented and informs the owner/operator when it needs to be refilled, or the temperature is too high is the first phase of IoT. This is a familiar example everyone understands. It's compelling, but only to a point. The data created by the sensors, in this example, is simply used by the program associated with the servicing operation. The industry is beginning to see examples of enhanced data for richer applications, which you might nominally call the second phase. Here, the historical data on the operation and usage of the machine is collected, along with the historical information on the temperature of the machine, inventory levels and mix, location, and even the forms of payment. By collecting this information, the owner/operator can do a much better job understanding what's going on, as well as, to some degree, why it's going on. They can begin to model what will go on, and begin to adapt to the changing circumstances to optimize everything from the servicing to the content to the energy used. This is still a closed-loop system, but it becomes data-rich, and with that, the information that's gathered and the decisions that can be made are improved.

The "utility value of the data" takes this a step further. The data can be abstracted from the system of origin. It's not that the information generated from the sensors on the Coke machine goes away. It doesn't. However, that same data can be cleansed and enriched and provided to a master data repository, where it might be combined with weather or environmental data, traffic data, demographic data, health data, and more. The combination of the variety of data can work to further enhance, sometimes to a great degree, the original application (in this case the Coke machine operation application), but it can also be used for other disparate applications consuming that same data, as well as a variety of other data to enhance the effectiveness of those applications. This data can also be used to service a common set of analytic tools, ranging from operational analytics (what is going on?) to investigative analytics (why is it going on?) to predictive analytics (what will go on?) and ultimately feed machine-learning algorithms to create truly adaptive systems. Last, the same set, or subset of underlying data can service other (non-IoT) applications in an enterprise like CRM or ERP, enhancing their value as well.

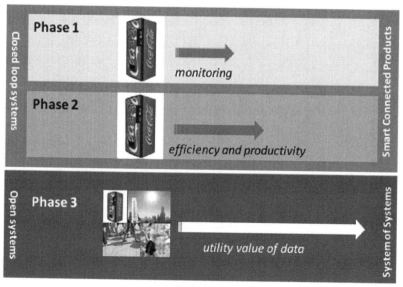

FIGURE 8.1

By approaching the baseline data from a utility standpoint, the reach and effectiveness of any singular bit of data can be multiplied as it enhances the ability to see emergent patterns that might otherwise remain opaque. It is a situation where the whole is greater than the sum of the parts. In the case of the Internet of Things, the parts are plentiful, the outlook is extreme, and the leverage to be gained by exploiting the utility value of the data is nothing short of tremendous. We don't yet understand what thresholds we will cross, what discoveries will be made, or the adaptive systems of tomorrow, but it is almost certain these gains will be directly tied to leveraging the utility value of this data.

What is the utility value of data?

To explore the utility value of data, it's helpful to understand how databases have evolved, and the key underlying thesis behind the creation of relational databases. In the early days of computing, data was generally either stored in flat files and tied directly to consuming programs or stored in hierarchical database structures, like IBM's IMS, that were also tied narrowly to specific applications, most notably ones associated with banking and telecommunications. The advantages here were that it didn't take a great deal of computing (relatively speaking) and was fast (again, relatively speaking). As people began to store more data and as they became more sophisticated in their understanding of the power associated with the underlying data, they began to look for an approach to better leverage this data.

This was fundamental to the creation of relational databases. The idea was to separate the creation of data from the consumption of data, thereby allowing organizations to leverage the utility value of that data. For instance, Citibank may be capturing all your banking transactions, such as you writing a check or making an ATM withdrawal. That transaction might be a record containing your account number, the amount of the check or ATM transaction, the identifier of the account, the routing of the transaction, the time and date of the transaction, etc. If the data is directly tied to the demand deposit accounting system, it is used to keep an accurate account of your money and ensure funds are moved correctly. If the data is stored in a relational database, then the DDA system can use it, but that ten or fifteen other applications might access the same information. Simply put, relational databases were designed to leverage the utility value of data.

The key is the notion of leveraging utility value of data. If data of all types—ranging from a banking transaction or the booking of an airline ticket or the purchase of groceries to demographic data like census information to the creation of machine-generated data like call data records or network log events—can then be stored in a manner that allows for a variety of applications to recognize the existence of that data and then consume it in a manner that suits the application, the power of any specific piece of data is far, far greater than if it were specifically tied to one application. The more the concept caught on and more enterprises began to utilize this data, the market began to see a battle of sorts being drawn between those running transactional systems (store operations, for example) and those utilizing the data for analytics (marketing, for example, looking for patterns in the data to drive their marketing plans). Performance and resources drove this. The more marketing people ran analytics, the slower the operational systems became and the more irritated operations people were. And the more data that was collected, the larger the impact was on the underlying resources. In the mid-nineties, the market began to see the rise of the idea of columnar databases as a standard for analytics. While standard row-based databases like Oracle, Sybase, and others were good for executing transactions and putting data into databases (writing a transition record), column-oriented relational databases were good for getting information out (read thousands of transaction records joined with other information). Examples of these early analytic databases were KDB, Sybase IQ, and RedBrick, and the technology continued to evolve to accommodate more and more data, with columnar databases becoming the standard for analytic data.

In more recent years we have seen the evolution of cloud computing and the emergence of NoSQL databases. What was once a crazy idea—that companies would trust their information to another company running their applications "in the cloud"—has become the norm. With that approach has come new considerations around data management. This doesn't mean relational databases have gone away, or that the utility value of the data is a concept now forgotten, but the amount of data, especially under these more modern deployment schemes, has grown even greater. In addition, as social media grew in prominence and other Internet applications began to take hold, we began to see significant growth in unstructured data such as blogs and commentary on Facebook, pictures and videos on YouTube, and much, much more. While relational databases had become the predominant venue for storing structured data for business applications, new entrants to the market like Apache Foundation's Hadoop, Cassandra, MongoDB, and other NoSQL solutions began to emerge as the new standard for what the industry has come to characterize as "data lakes," where all your data gets put "into the lake" and then you have a variety of methods for pulling it out for use.

The emergence of NoSQL databases is meant to accommodate massive, petabyte scale storage of data, but with certain accommodations. With scale comes trade-offs, even with the underlying continued acceleration of hardware capabilities. NoSQL databases generally see that trade-off in the form of "eventual consistency" and in the area of complex analytics across various databases. So while NoSQL is highly scalable, distributed, very flexible (you can throw "anything" into the data lake), and generally lower cost (open source software and commodity hardware), there are usually limitations on how data can be joined together. It generally requires an increased need for developers and database designers, and while it guarantees availability, it doesn't guarantee consistency, so there are some applications that are not suited for this. As with anything, there are always pros and cons, but the market in general has clearly embraced cloud computing and the use of NoSQL.

Databases have clearly evolved from the early days of tying the data to the application. The notion of the utility value of the data is hardly new. Yet, early IoT subsystems generally tie the sensors to the consuming application, usually in the form of an application associated with a particular IoT-enabled product. In this regard, it's like the early days of mainframe computing. However, as people and organizations begin to appreciate that the most meaningful value of IoT is to be derived from the data, the lesson learned from many years ago will be applied to IoT architecture. Specifically, the creation of the IoT data will be separated from the consumption of the IoT data. With this very simple concept will come an astronomical amount of additional value driven by IoT.

Why is the utility value of data important?

While we remain impressed and intrigued by the many, many variations of IoT devices and offerings entering the market, and most readily confess that fans that talk to thermostats that can be remotely controlled by iPhones, as well as Fitbits linked to diet tracking and cars that can tell you when you are drifting into another lane are all compelling. The early "compelling factor" is destined to be overwhelmed by something much greater. At the epicenter of this isn't so much the devices themselves as the data. We will see the evolution of the Internet of Things evolve in three not so distinct phases all pointed at leveraging the utility value of the data. If anything, the insight gained from the data, holistically, is the Holy Grail. So what's the utility value of the data and why should we care?

Let's start with the basic systems. As discussed previously, the closed-loop message-response system where an IoT-enabled product ("Smart Connected Product" in Heppleman-Porter parlance) is deployed. This is the first of the three phases. This is where the sensor data is directly tied to the consumption of that data. The product manufacturer gets the data; the data provides the product manufacturer strong leverage. They can service the product better. They can develop stickier relationships. They can make more money. And you'll be okay with this because you have a better product and better service relationship.

The second phase is marked by the growing recognition of the value of the data. In many cases, this starts with the very closed-loop message response systems we have just discussed. The smart connected product provider begins to realize that collecting and analyzing that data has greater value, especially for predictive maintenance, but also for product design and other analysis. So they collect the data. This is a very basic, albeit important step forward, and most of the IoT market has long been here as well. The second part of this entails the sharing of the data, and this is the critical step. Once the data is recognized as being valuable, there is also growing recognition that the data is valuable in the context of other related IoT products and the data from those products. For example, the information coming from the IoT-enabled HVAC, thermostat, window blinds, and ceiling fans all have relevance to each other. This would be the "Product System" connecting the systems

Users of IoT systems tend to approach things based on what they know, but the challenge is to think differently. People may think "that can't be done", but then figure out it can. This is the paradigm shift that must occur, but it can be tough. A lot of traditional thinking is rooted in existing business processes. In some ways, early IoT solutions then seem like a solution looking for a problem to solve. If you can invert that, however, and start by asking "if all the data were available, then what would we do?", then that changes the equation. We need to untether.

— Matt Jennings

Regional President, Americas Bosch Software Innovations

together and allowing them to share information makes them all better. Google Nest engaged a partnership with Big Ass Fans. This was no accident. An integrated product system isn't a zero-sum gain. They are more powerful and valuable when linked. And so, the information should be integrated and shared. This is a very good step. However, the lens on this is still largely focused on the product providers, but the cracks begin to show. The smart home battleground is most telling. There were many products pushed out to the market that were IoT-enabled smart home products that used different protocols and governed by different control systems that simply would not work together. The home-owner wanting a smart home found it difficult to reconcile this. To some extent this remains the case, but large corporate initiatives like Apple Homekit, Google Nest, Samsung SmartThings and others are beginning to deliver easier-to-configure solutions and use total home integration. On a higher level, you are seeing groups like the AllSeen Alliance working to drive open standards to address the proprietary solution approach, and this, in many ways, foreshadows the broader market direction. A market that naturally needs to interconnect also needs established standards and rules that everyone can understand. This has been the case for telecommunications, energy delivery, lighting, plumbing, and most forms of infrastructure.

The third phase is leveraging the utility value of data, and it is so important because it will allow the full leverage of the Internet of Things. It is the most important pathway to insight. It is also easy to see coming if you consider the progression of IoT. Two years ago, you may have had a Nest Thermostat or Fitbit. Today you may have three or four systems in your home linked, and your Fitbit may be tied to health apps and other health-related devices like a smart scale or smart blood pressure machine. But five years out, how many more IoT-enabled devices do you think you'll be using? Will this be at home? Will it be at work? Will it be on the way to work? The extent to which IoT devices will be deployed will be far-reaching, and the need for and level of integration will be, by necessity, much, much greater. To do this, deployment architecture should change. Think of this as that the "lens" to "see the data" must move from the eyes of simply the product provider to the eyes of the buyers and users of these systems. In other words, instead of the view being form the lighting vendor, or kitchen equipment vendor, or HVAC vendor, it will be from the view of SeaLand, or Disney, or Target, or McDonalds.

In doing this, the creation of the IoT data will be abstracted from the consumption of the IoT data. At its most basic level, this will allow for the proper cleansing, enriching, filtering, aggregating, and supplementation of the data. The fifteen different systems gathering data at the fast food restaurant will also merge in point of sale, crew scheduling, inventory data, and external demographic data, weather data, and new data provided by the city about pedestrian traffic, street vehicle traffic, air quality, luminosity and other data that fortifies what becomes the data signature for a wide variety of consuming applications both locally, remotely within the enterprise, and externally to remote constituents who have a need to all or part of the data being collected and enriched.

Think about it this way: with holistic data gathering—gathering data in greater depth across a broader range of inputs for a longer period—you can see patterns and gain insights that would otherwise be obscured. When you have a very thorough examination, your doctor will not only listen to you breathe and tap your knee to check your reflexes, she will have all kinds of blood work and other tests run, up to and including things like stress tests and EKGs. More data is better. But it is usually costly, intrusive, and seldom readily available to the average person. The key is to somehow make it easier and more cost effective to get that data. This is the "Big Data" idea. Sometimes the emergent patterns that make a difference are revealed by the correlation of lots of different data. Understanding your blood pressure, even over a longer period with greater granularity may still reveal limited information. Combining that information with blood sugar levels, temperature, steps taken, food ingested, and even external information like ambient temperature or pollen counts or other air quality metrics can be combined for potentially much richer, more effective digital signatures that paint a very telling story, and perhaps a very accurate predictive story that can trigger action to prevent illness. For the human body, this will soon include a person's genomic scan (as the cost of doing this drops to a truly affordable level) thereby providing a digital signature and related insight that would have been unimaginable a generation ago. The key is to gain the maximum insight to take the best actions possible, regardless of the situation in question. Leveraging the utility value of the data provides that ability._

To deploy IOT systems without leveraging the utility value of the data is like owning a car where you can only use it without passengers, and only drive it between four specified locations. It would have value, but the value would be incredibly (and ridiculously) limited compared to what everyone would expect. IoT systems that are closed-loop message-response systems would have the same limitations. And rightfully, the market will not stand for this. But to effectively leverage the utility value of the data, you must employ the right IoT architecture, which we will explore next.

The Importance of Having the
Right Deployment Architecture

The right deployment architecture can mean everything. It can be the difference between effectively providing the right data at the right time to the right place and spending too much while simultaneously limiting the value, reach, and leverage of the data. Think about how important it is that a house be architected thoughtfully, where the bathrooms and hallways and general use rooms and bedrooms all work well together. Now rearrange that architecture randomly and you end up with hallways going nowhere, inaccessible bedrooms, bathrooms that make no sense, and underling infrastructure that costs too much to reach places that also don't make sense. A bad IoT architecture is like that, on steroids. That said, there is no silver bullet.

There are a number of factors contributing to the increased emphasis on using the right IoT architecture. One is the maturity of the market and people gaining a better understanding that the right architecture means greater leverage. Another is the importance and value associated with properly leveraging the utility value of the data and thus highlighting the need to either own or at least access and control this data. Another is the obvious imperative to secure these systems. For these reasons and more, organizations will place an increasing emphasis on IoT architecture.

This is a departure from a one-off view of putting IoT-enabled systems into play. The emphasis on the right deployment architecture is a reflection of the growing maturity of the market, and elements ranging from the role of edge processing, distributed clouds and central clouds, sensor choices, network choices, when and where to persist data, how to effectively propagate the right data to the right constituents in the right manner are all elements in the large equation. As organizations begin to grasp the enormous value to be gained by properly and thoughtfully incorporating IoT, these considerations will pay dividends.

Leverage starts with the right architecture. This begins with the abstraction of the creation of the IoT data from the consumption. This allows you to re-use any piece of data for a variety of consuming applications, thereby generating greater leverage. The most obvious architectural choice will be an event-driven, publish, and subscribe architecture.

What are deployment architectures and why should you care?

At a high level, the deployment architecture is the reference framework for how the information flows from the point of origin to the point of consumption. There are a variety of choices and corresponding considerations. To determine what is "right" one needs to understand the various considerations, starting with the most basic technology deployment architectural choices. The three most obvious choices would be a monolithic architecture, a distributed but centrally managed architecture, or a distributed peer-based architecture. Deployment architectures have evolved quite a bit, especially with the overwhelming movement to cloud computing. Now we are seeing the role of micro-services becoming increasingly important, as well as the role of edge computing, especially for the Internet of Things. Let's start with a quick look at fairly standard approaches, then look more closely at some of the additional architectural considerations.

Monolithic Architecture

Traditionally, a monolithic architecture would have been identified with mainframe computing. In the early days of mainstream computing (1970s and 80s), companies would typically work with mainframe computers, where the users worked from CICS terminals or some equivalent. IBM was the predominant player, but Honeywell, Sperry-Univac, Burroughs, and Cray (to some extent) were all players in the mainframe market. Notable was also the presence of Hitachi and Amdahl, the IBM "Plug Compatible" players offering mainframes that would run the IBM MVS Operating System. In this environment, the terminals (often called "green screens" for their green LED character-based screens) were attached to the central computer. There was central control. The applications were all run centrally, and internal development staff developed most of them. The business applications were mostly written in Cobol, and the engineering applications were generally written in Fortran. Information technology operations were "glass houses," known for the large data centers that were often inside glass walls, in part so "outsiders" could revel at the enormous computing capabilities of the organization.

Most of the early systems used hierarchical databases, especially IBM's IMS, and these were usually directly tied to the consuming applications, so the data and the application were basically isolated. As we moved to the mid-eighties and later, the market began to see the emergence of relational databases. This began almost a decade earlier with the System-R team from IBM working on the early versions of what would become DB2. Oracle, Ingress, and a few others were also beginning to show up in the market. The extremely important architectural implication of the relational databases was the separation of the creation of the data from the consumption of the data. While this started in the mainframe world, it quickly spilled over into client server computing.

In the vein of what's old is new again, today, centralized, monolithic architecture takes the form of the centralized cloud where most, if not all processing is done centrally. There is clearly a trend in the market, starting years ago, but picking up huge momentum in the market, for virtualized applications that are deployed through centralized cloud offerings. Salesforce.com is an icon of SaaS (software-as-a-service) offerings. At the highest level, the architecture is fairly simple. All the data and almost all of the processing happen in the centralized cloud. This has taken off to the point that all major technology stack companies have a large stake in cloud-based offerings, ranging from IBM to HP to SAP to Oracle, and most notably, Amazon. For the purposes of this discussion, we will view a monolithic architecture as a monolithic cloud-based, virtualized application.

The arguments for a monolithic architecture include control of the application and a single support function. Basically, the application is the application. The provider controls the environment and the code-line, and everyone running the monolithic application is running the exact same code. A user may have the option of configuring their use for their needs, but the same application is still running for everyone. This means the need for distributing code and the complexing of supporting that code on different operating systems, hardware, and potentially even different databases and other components goes away entirely. And the code can evolve at the pace of the supplier uninhibited by the constraints associated with on-premise deployed applications where customer A may move at a pace three times slower than customer B for upgrading to the newest version.

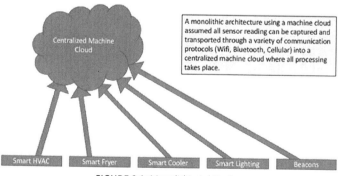

A monolithic architecture using a machine cloud assumed all sensor reading can be captured and transported through a variety of communication protocols (Wifi, Bluetooth, Cellular) into a centralized machine cloud where all processing takes place.

FIGURE 9.1: Monolithic Achitecture

The arguments against this is a heavy approach that has certain reliance's that are unacceptable and that it lends itself to becoming unwieldy over time. For instance, if the architecture relies on connectivity to the cloud, and the connectivity goes down for any reason, you are lost. It is safe to say that connectivity is getting better and better. Yet, if you are operating in a remote area, this may not be something you take for granted. Also, monolithic architectures are typically constructed of multiple tiers, including the GUI (graphical user interface) layer, the application layer, the network/middleware layer, and data layer. One you lock these into the architecture, it can become increasingly difficult to make changes to the component technologies, thereby limiting your flexibility moving forward. Experience suggests this can get complex and messy over time, and more and more changes, features, and functions are added and the component isolation begins to bleed into a more difficult set of code with complex and difficult interdependencies.

Also, scaling these solutions can be difficult. If they share a single data store, sometimes this can be limiting as the data volumes and complexity increase. But again, you are somewhat locked into the architecture, so it isn't easy to rewrite one of the tiers with different technology. It can also be tough to roll out. The deployment velocity can be hampered based on dependencies, although this is a two-edged sword, as there are also elements of the rollout that are accommodated well by this approach, like the continuity of the experience amongst the various users and the consistency of the training requirements.

Examples of this that we all know would be Facebook, LinkedIn, and most social media applications. It would also be (to a high degree) Salesforce.com, Workday, or many other successful SaaS applications.

In the context of IoT, this would be the Axeda Machine Cloud (now a part of PTC/Thingworx) or the Ayla Networks Platform or any of the other platforms that tout easy capability to deploy their sensor instrumented, IoT-enabled products into their cloud service that makes it easy to do great things. In some ways, these claims are valid. This architecture is fundamentally simple. The issues come when you are trying to integrate what is basically a cloud-based silo into the larger enterprise. It can be done, but this does not come cheap or easy. Salesforce.com took over ten years to reach the market presence that was formidable enough that creating acceptable integration paths made sense in the context of other market offerings.

Distributed N-tier (centrally-controlled) architecture

Traditionally, a distributed but centrally-controlled architecture would have been identified as client server (basically a two-tiered architecture). In the early nineties, client server fast became the dominant architecture, where personal computers played a key role in offloading centralized processing and enabling knowledge workers in much more powerful ways. A good example might be the call center worker. When a call comes into the call center, the number could be picked up by the central server, but all the various servicing options from product information to scripts and calculators or client-based information could either be resident on the local client, or moved onto the local client at the commencement of the call. This gave the knowledge worker the ability to engage locally with more information at the fingertips of the call center agent, but did not rely on the connection to the central office or the associated processing power of (what would have then been) the centralized mainframe.

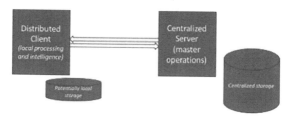

FIGURE 9.2: Client Server Architecture

Distributed architectures began to evolve as the progress in networking and departmental and personal computing improved. As the network capabilities increased and the cost of communications came down, the networks could realistically support distributed computing. And too, as the power associated with personal computers as well as departmental computers like those from Digital Equipment Corporation, Prime Computer, HP and others continued to increase, the idea of distributed computing went from being technologically possible but cost prohibitive, to the point where it was technologically and economically practical to do so. In fact, in some instances it became impractical to not do so.

The distributed computing architecture operated from an approach where there would be a single system of record and a centralized governance approach to applications, but the actual execution of the applications was distributed across the network utilizing distributed processing resources.

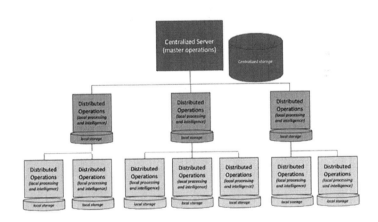

FIGURE 9.3: Distributed Computing Architecture

Today, this takes the form of or a more modern version characterized as a publish and subscribe architecture. Even this isn't so modern, but is based on the idea that there should be a separation between the creation of data and the consumption of data.

By approaching the architecture this way, there are a variety of benefits, but the key ones being it is flexible, adaptable, and leverages the data in the most aggressive way.

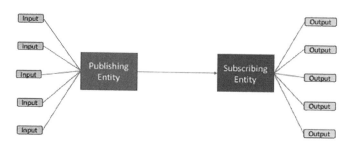

FIGURE 9.4: Basic Publish-Subscribe Architecture

The arguments for this are that applications can be both publishers and subscribers of information, allowing for maximum leverage (and sharing) of information that reaches beyond silos. This also lends to greater resiliency, as well as there can be multiple replicated hubs creating fault tolerance and high availability.

Realistically, the depiction in Figure 9.1 is unlikely. The more likely scenario would be several different applications that may be both producers and consumers of data. Let's look at an example. Entity A might be a smart HVAC System. Entity B could be a smart kitchen equipment system. Entity C might be a point-of-sale system, and Entity D could be an inventory system.

Each of these entities would publish certain types of data, as seen in Table 8.1. While the specific data being recorded by a given system will obvious differ, there could be insight derived from the correlation between the data coming from different IoT-enabled products. For instance, a temperature gauge is going to produce temperature readings, clear and simple. So, it goes with some of these operational systems.

	Data 1	Data 2	Data 3
A-HVAC	Target Temperature	Fan Speed	Outside Temperature
B-Low-Fat Fryer	Temperature	Utilization	Cycles
C-POS	Top Item	Unit Sales	Total Sales
D-Inventory	Items	Inv Count	Thaw Time

TABLE 9.1: Publishing Data

As these systems begin to operate as a part of an ecosystem, the applications become more sophisticated and powerful, and the inter-dependencies become more important, and more evident. The restaurant operator may gain insight from looking at the relationships between various assets and operational systems to make decisions. It might be determined that when the temperature outside gets beyond a certain point, the fan speed on the HVAC increases to max speed, after which it takes much longer to reach and maintain the target temperature. Under those conditions, they may further detect that the low-fat fryer utilization drops and the associated order for french fries drop as well. This, of course, would then be correlated to the inventory system, where demand in inventory can ultimately be tracked to outside temperatures. The models are likely to be far more sophisticated and involve far more data than this example, but the idea of leveraging data across multiple silos is the key.

The arguments against a distributed model are that it can be costlier to deploy and support, because it assumed you had more computational resources and more systems to be supported. There might be issues associated with lack of standards associated with element in the system (like store A having a Windows PC and store B having a Mac), therefore, not only requiring more administration, but more complexity to administrate. This could extend to additional security and high availability concerns as well. While there is no single point of failure to most distributed systems, backing up each individual entity within the architecture becomes more of an issue, whereas the central architecture readily handles this.

The most obvious example of this in the context of IoT would be fog computing, where a good deal of the computational work is pushed to the edge device. Examples of fog computing run broad, from oil and gas to retail to transportation, energy distribution, and more.

Distributed, peer-to-peer architecture and mesh networks

Architecturally, peer-to-peer is also a distributed architecture. The main difference here is that there is no central control. Peer-to-peer is organized around the concept of equal peer nodes where a given peer can be both a supplier and consumer of resources.[34] Peer-to-peer networks can be both structured and unstructured. An unstructured peer-to-peer network is formed by nodes that are autonomous, and randomly connect to other nodes. Structured peer-to-peer networks have a framework that governs the interaction between the peers. Each peer is still autonomous, but now they interoperate against a defined framework, driving greater efficiencies than what would exist in the unstructured network.

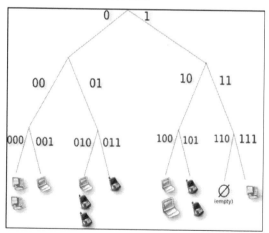

FIGURE 9.5

The arguments for this are the flexibility of the system and resiliency, as well as the ability for users to work autonomously

---

34 https://en.wikipedia.org/wiki/Peer-to-peer.

without many (or any) limitations. This has been especially true for content delivery, as made famous by Naptser for music sharing. However, that also led to issues regarding copyright violations and other contractual issues. So notwithstanding what the technology can do, the business issues associated with some of the content delivery capabilities using this architecture have been problematic. However, this is proving to be a favored approach for distribution of content by a growing number of projects in the public domain, where the copyright issues don't exist.

The arguments against this start with security. With peer-to-peer networks, the connectivity can ostensibly be established with anyone. And while there can be safeguards built into how this happens, like proper authentication, concerns still exist (as do many examples) regarding security breaches by those on the network or even those producing the products that form the basics of a given application, especially ones based on IoT devices. There are numerous examples of IP based security cameras being hacked and having the content, of the parking lot attendant's booth, of your office, and of the baby monitor being broadcast over the Internet without your permission. The well-publicized case of Foscam, the Chinese security camera manufacturer, highlights this in spades.[35]

Many people equate Mesh Networks to peer-to-peer networks. They are certainly similar. While peer-to-peer networks will often utilize an existing infrastructure and follow a tree structure, mesh networks add nodes as incremental elements connecting directly into the network, where the new connections add additional resiliency to the network. In the context of networking, peer-to-peer generally equates to ad hoc, self-organizing networks, whereas mesh networks infer bridge-to-bridge or router-to-router, with many to many connectivity relationships and no central hub.[36]

In the context of IoT, one of the key notions of mesh networking is the ability for a given node to ingest and propagate

35 https://www.hackable.io/blog/how-p2p-becoming-iot-nightmare.
36 http://superuser.com/questions/481145/what-is-the-difference-between-ad-hoc-and-mesh-network-also-with-p2p.

messages from other nodes. This has meaningful implications to leveraging low power networks supporting devices with low data rates and with particularly long battery life and in a highly reliable fashion. IoT applications that need to rely on these capabilities range from industrial process monitoring to fence line/border security to smart parking solutions and more.[37] One other particularly interesting use case for mesh networking is autonomous driving, or even with connected cars that are not completely autonomous. The idea here is that each car broadcasts to the cars around them, forming a network that is dynamically adapting to the cares in proximity, communicating presence and speed and other relevant driving information.

Architecture relative to market direction

Now let's look at the practicality of how the Internet of Things will evolve. This means thinking through the likely progression of IoT in the context of what's accessible and affordable against a backdrop of security, governance, data leverage, and economic considerations. In doing so, there are a few considerations worth noting. Specifically:

- Closed-loop, message-response silos will give way to deployment architectures designed to leverage the utility value of the data. This means the ten or so IoT subsystems running in a retail store or fast food restaurant or a factory will not be viewed in isolation, but rather in the context of the other silos. It will further incorporate other operational systems (like scheduling, point-of-sale, inventory, etc.) and ultimately external data like demographic data, street IoT data, weather data, etc. Together this broader set of data can be cleansed, enriched, and exposed to consuming applications as well as an analytic workbench consisting of operational, investigative, and predictive analytics as well as machine learning.

37 http://cds.linear.com/docs/en/article/Mesh_Network_Protocols_for_IoT.pdf.

First Level IoT: Most IoT Deployments are centered around capital equipment and are closed loop silos

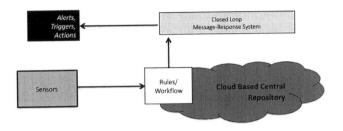

Data is mostly owned and controlled by the vendors

FIGURE 9.6: Closed-Loop Message-Response System

- **The role of edge processing will increase dramatically.** The implication is they're the point of ingestion and initial processing of a variety of IoT-enabled end points, where the initial processing, filtering, alerting and triggering, as well as certain computational work will be accomplished.

They will (often and soon) need to accommodate Edge Processing

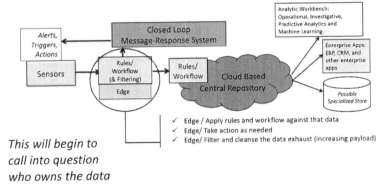

FIGURE 9.7: Edge Computing Considerations

- **Contemplation of servicing multiple constituencies will drive an event-driven, publish-subscribe architecture in most cases.** The reason is simple. Once the sensor messages are captured at the edge (ostensibly the *first receiver*), there will be a variety of other constituencies with a need to consume that data, either in atomic or enriched form. This can range from regional and corporate offices to capital equipment providers to regulatory agencies, trading partners, and more. A key element of this will be the notion that at any point in the ecosystem, the utility value of the underlying data will be leveraged for the benefit of that constituent. The store has one view. The regional operations offices have another. The corporate offices have another, as do the capital equipment provider, the regulatory oversight and compliance office, and the supply chain partner. Ten different parties for ten different reasons might consume that one temperature reading or beacon message. That's a good thing.

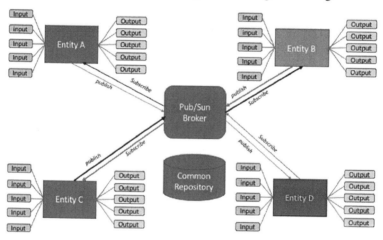

FIGURE 9.8: Publish and Subscribe Architecture

- **Governance will become critical, along with security.** Because various constituencies will require atomic or enriched data in a variety of ways for a variety of reasons, governance considerations regarding data become critical. Who owns the data? Who is the steward of the data? Who can see data, to what degree? How are these permissions managed? How is the security established and enforced? Right now, the main infrastructure consideration we hear about is security. Some are more concerned than others (the smartest being the most concerned), but there is little being discussed today in most circles about the other governance considerations. As the awareness of the power of the underlying data increases, the demand for broader consumption of that data will increase and the governance considerations will become increasingly important. This is going to happen.

- **A huge opportunity will be the analytics and associated emerging applications on top of this architecture, including machine learning.** It will be an increasingly sophisticated analytic workbench. It will be the new restaurant chain operational optimization application. It will be the holistic healthcare monitoring and alerting system that includes webRTC interfaces with nurses and physicians via Telehealth services.

The right architecture is focused on taking what's technologically possible and making it practical by making it accessible and affordable. This can be done. And when it is—when the exponentially increased volumes of IoT data can be harnessed and leveraged across a broad range of constituents easily and cost effectively, the benefits will be enormous. But before these benefits can be realized, we must move down this path.

Other considerations

There are other elements that should be considered. It is interesting to hear other people discuss certain elements of the ecosystem and how they consider, or don't consider the impact. For example, "Storage is almost free," "This has limited scalability," "Network bandwidth is so affordable and available," and other myths that sound good to someone who either doesn't want to think or simply doesn't know what they're talking about. It is true that storage costs have dropped, network bandwidth capabilities have increased, the cost of bandwidth has dropped, and scalability has increased for data and computational needs, but to suggest these aren't considerations is wrong. Worse yet, the part that is left out of the equation time and time again is the human capital associated with establishing and maintaining these systems. Again, architecture is everything. But for now, let's just look closer at the profound impact having the right deployment architecture can make on the network, both from a technological and business standpoint. While this isn't meant to be an in-depth look at all specific elements within an IoT architecture, it's worth touching on a few other key considerations.

Sensors

Since the Internet of Things is first and foremost about gaining an understanding of "things," this "understanding" speaks to knowing the state of a given object or asset, like a windmill, a car, a shipping container, or even your own body. In short, the sensor is possibly the most important element enabling the IoT. These sensors are telling us what the temperature or vibration or acceleration of a given device is at a given time. They measure moisture content or the presence of certain gasses. They can tell us when there is a moving object in proximity of the sensor, or when the noise level goes up or down.

Sensors are getting more and more powerful, able to detect a variety of conditions that were more narrowly scoped before. They are also getting smaller, and more power efficient, so the life of a given sensor may be much longer now, and the size may be much smaller (allowing for better configurability), while the capabilities have increased. Designing your architecture to take advantage of advances in sensor technology is key. To the extent you can plug in new sensors, and unplug older ones, your IoT environment can advance readily and cost effectively.

Network considerations

It goes without saying that the network is a key consideration for the IoT. There are a variety of network options at play in any IoT architecture. The decisions made about the network will differ depending on the use case. For instance, network considerations relative wearable devices will be different than smart streetlights and different still from the connected cars driving underneath. Some connectivity may be through wired devices with Ethernet connectivity, and other may be via wireless devices using a variety of protocols. Some devices will connect behind an edge device, while others may use a SIM card connecting directly into a Cloud. Some devices will have distance limitations, where device proximity allows or eliminates the usability of the device.

	TCP/IP Support	Gateway Needed?	Power	Data Rate	Topology	Wireless Spectrum	Alliance	Module Costs (5K EAU)	Other
Ethernet	Over 802.3	No, directly wired to Internet	High / Power-over-Ethernet (PoE) 802.3af	Up to 1 Gbps	Varies	None	None	$10 +	RJ45
Wi-Fi	Over 802.11	No, connects to Internet through Wi-Fi access points and routers	High (low-power modules available for battery applications)	1-135 Mbps	None	2.4 GHz, 5 GHz	Wi-Fi Alliance	< $10 +	Internal or external antenna
6LoWPAN	Over 802.15.4	Yes	Low	0.04-0.25 Mbps	Varies	868-921 MHz, 2.4 GHz	Internet Engineering Task Force (IETF)	$5 +	Internal or external antenna
ZigBee	Lacks native TCP/IP support, based on 802.15.4	Yes, ZigBee Coordinator	Low	0.04-0.25 Mbps	Mesh	868-921 MHz, 2.4 GHz	ZigBee Alliance	< $4 +	Internal or external antenna
Z-Wave	Lacks native TCP/IP support, based on Z-Wave standard	Yes	Low	0.1 Mbps, primarily for remote control	Mesh	868-921 MHz	Z-Wave Alliance	$5 +	Internal or external antenna, managed by Sigma Designs
Bluetooth	Lacks native TCP/IP support, based on Bluetooth standard	Yes	Moderate	0.7-2.1 Mbps	Point-to-point	2.4 GHz	Bluetooth Special Interest Group (SIG)	$5 +	Pairing can be complicated, max 8 devices in piconet, ~100 ms latency
Bluetooth Smart (such as BLE, BT 4.0)	Lacks native TCP/IP support, based on Bluetooth LE standard	Yes	Low to moderate	0.27 Mbps maximum	Point-to-point	2.4 GHz	Bluetooth Special Interest Group (SIG)	$5 +	Simpler to pair devices, new version 4.2 connects directly with Internet
Cellular	TCP/IP over cellular network	No, connects to Internet/cloud through cellular service provider network	High	Varies based on technology	Point-to-point	Varies	None	Monthly service charges, modules, carrier certification fees	External Antenna Only, Monthly Service

TABLE 9.2: Networking Considerations

It's also important to consider how the network relates to the overall architecture required for a given entity or solutions. For instance, if you are running a factory and you want to have machines that are IoT enabled sitting behind a *first receiver*/Gateway; it will be important to ensure all devices can interface with the gateway. It's true that many gateways in the market provide for multiple protocols and connectivity options to coexist; it's desirable they link together as seamlessly, as cost effectively, and as securely as possible. As the market matured, certain industry groups have arisen to drive networking standards that aim to make this easier, like the WIFI Alliance, ZigBee Alliance, Zwave Alliance, and Bluetooth Special Interest Group.

Also, another key consideration is the power consumption associated with network choices. This can guide whether certain use cases make sense for certain choices. For instance, a wearable device needs lower power requirements and wireless connectivity.

Lastly, there are various cost characteristics associated with the networking choices. High cost choices are less likely to be viable for low-end devices whereas they may have the perfect attributes for high value assets needing greater resources.

Cloud computing

There are certainly some organizations that view cloud computing as synonymous with the Internet of Things. In fact, it is reasonable to assume most people expect some inclusion of either a public or private cloud in any IoT architecture. Cloud computing has evolved steadily over the years from the early days when SaaS vendors like Salesforce.com came on the scene with cloud-based sales force automation to where we are today where major technology vendors like Oracle, SAP, IBM, Microsoft, Cisco, and others have fundamentally pivoted their business to Cloud-based, virtualized services for software (SaaS), infrastructure (IaaS), platforms (PaaS), and even data (DaaS). This is a fundamental shift in how people and organizations view computing resources and suggest we have evolved from the day where few trusted the cloud as a viable option to a point where most believe it is the best viable option.

As this progression has emerged, not only have big tech suppliers changed direction, but we have seen giants emerge, most notable Amazon, with Amazon Web Services (AWS), as the predominant cloud services provider. At the same time Amazon and other companies moved progressively to the cloud, IoT has continued to evolve, and the role of the cloud in IoT looms large. Amazon has their AWS IoT offering. PTC acquired Thingworx, Axeda, Cold Light, and others, where the primary architecture assumes the centralized Cloud repository. This is true, as expected, of AWS IoT as well, although even there, AWS has now acknowledged the importance of edge processing as an important element of some (perhaps most) architectural delivery models.

Some would argue the cost and flexibility of cloud computing has been driven so low that the corresponding drop in costs and increase in bandwidth for networking has created the scenario where it may seem perfectly reasonable and acceptable to many organizations to have every sensor push messages directly into the cloud. The counter-arguments against this run far and wide, but certainly the notion of the role of the cloud in an IoT architecture is a given for many. But it isn't for all. In the industrial space, there are operations that are still reluctant to have their data flow "away from the factory." There is capital equipment, never intended to be used while connected to the Internet, being reconfigured to participate in IoT networks, but still largely confined to limited reach. Hitachi Lumada is an interesting platform that contemplated being deployed in the cloud directly, with no cloud at all, or in hybrid or virtual environments. As a design point they specifically made Lumada capable of a wide variety of deployment options such that the network reliance's did not become an impediment to implementation.

Data (and scale) considerations

As the IoT continues to gain momentum, there can be no denying that the volume of data associated with it will skyrocket. While projection after projection may differ as to exact amounts, they are all consistent in suggesting the numbers will be huge. Much of this data is structured data generated by a wide variety of sensors, but IoT also involves a variety of other unstructured data as well. Structured and unstructured, this data is like a plentiful oil reserve, full of value but not always easy to mine. Yet, as with oil, the benefits can be significant.

This data provides significantly increased granularity, both from existing data points, like asset location at a given point in time, as well as an increasing amount of net new, complimentary data, like everything from operating temperatures to acceleration to moisture contents and much, much more. With this increased breadth and depth of data, more specific insights can be gained, issues can be understood and addressed more quickly, and predictions can increase in precision.

CIOs, along with their operational counterparts are collectively realizing that this data can decrease operational costs, increase customer retention, enhance product development, and increase service opportunities to the point of new business models. What once was a product sale might now be a subscription based on outcomes, like "lighting as a service." There are smaller companies outpacing larger more established ones, and older companies reinventing themselves. Yet, the IoT remains relatively new, and the overall penetration is most likely still in its infancy. This is because most of the IoT subsystems are still relatively siloed, and the data is often used by one or limited numbers of constituents. But this will change.

As IoT matures, organizations will begin to embrace the notion of leveraging the utility value of the data. Where a system might have contemplated data from one IoT subsystem, it may soon be working with fifteen sets of IoT data to be evaluated in the context of one another. Moreover, the enhanced signatures derived from internally operated IoT systems will likely be complimented by a significantly increased set of external data provided by local governments, supply chain partners, or other third parties. As this happens, the growth in data will be enormous. This is good and bad. Mountains of data can mean mountains of opportunity, but this is where the distinction between what's technologically possible and what's actually practical becomes paramount.

We have seen a move towards things like Hadoop and Spark

(both open source offerings from the Apache Foundation) that have great strengths in terms of scaling, but come with certain limitations regarding how to administer the environments, interrogate the data, and manage the overall operating costs. In the context of IoT, NoSQL databases are becoming the de facto standards for centralized data lakes, but the role of standard relational and analytic relational databases won't quickly go away. This is especially true since the IoT world is filled with machine-generated data like sensor readings, which work very well with structured databases, especially one that handle time series effectively. That said, the unstructured data found in images, videos (think security cameras, medical equipment, etc.) work very well with various NoSQL databases.

As we continue to move forward, and these systems become so much more prevalent, the volume will grow to points that would have been hard to imagine even five years ago. Let's assume we are looking at several different multi-petabyte datasets where an organization wants to interrogate that data with complex queries. Is that possible? Of course, the answer is yes. But investigative analytics with datasets this large where the interrogation spans multiple petabyte plus datasets isn't an easy or cheap process. These would be the very long running queries that take hours and huge amounts of resources and depending on the use case, the results might only serve to tell you if you are even on the right track. This mass accumulation of data will point to a likely accommodation to bring what is technologically possible into the realm of what's practical. Said differently, if it takes hours or days to get to actionable insight, then the value of taking that action may well be lost. The challenge becomes speed to insight.

The likely answer to this challenge is a technological accommodation. Just like vast NoSQL environments began to use the notion of eventual consistency in their file systems (think Facebook or Linked-In), organizations will likely adjust to the notion of eventual accuracy based on leveraging metadata. Metadata, in the form of statistical models, can be used to drive high value approximations in a fraction of the time with a fraction of the resources. Unlike sampling (which does have merit is some situations), a statistical metadata-driven approach, unlike sampling, will be viable across more complex environments and not suffer from degraded sample erosion or missed outliers, so the validity of the results can be compelling. So what does this mean? Mountains of data are sure to come. The trick will be mining the data under the surface to gain insight within a timeframe and associated cost to make this practical

The importance of the edge

Edge computing, sometimes in the form of a "fog computing architecture" is a key piece of this and can be consistent with an event-driven, publish, and subscribe architecture. There are a multitude of reasons this makes sense in many cases.

First and most obvious, the edge is the muffler for data exhaust. "Data exhaust" refers to the messages that ultimately have no real value. Everyone seems to agree that the machine data generated by sensors will be plentiful. But because there are so many sensor readings, doesn't mean each reading is valuable. In fact, in many instances, nearly all messages are inconsequential. For instance, if you take the temperature in every room in a 1000 room building every second, and you are also polling CO_2, luminosity, noise, and occupancy, and you planned to retain the data for thirty days, you would be keeping 12.94 billion messages. But the temperature (or CO_2 readings, or luminosity, noise, or occupancy) readings just don't change that often. Sometimes even when they do change it doesn't change enough to trigger any relevant threshold. It is likely that 99 percent or more of the data ingested in this use case can be thrown out. Moreover, you should want to throw it out. The reason is simple: the noise to signal ratio is too high with a high data exhaust rate. If you can filter out the inconsequential messages at the edge, you increase the value of the payload you deliver to central processing. You also spend less to get it there and less to keep it there. Your analysis of what is there is more powerful by virtue of the fact that adding needless data, in orders of magnitude, isn't unduly challenging the analytics.

Cost is another factor that supports this approach. Most aren't looking to spend as much as possible. There are many instances where edge processing won't save you money. But there are certainly others where it will, and possibly in a big way. This is a function of network traffic, additional central storage, additional compute power, and additional personnel. This is especially true if your message stream has a high exhaust rate.

Last, latency may be an issue contributing to the benefit of edge processing. Most IoT implementations will ultimately be as much or more about the utility value of the data than alerting and triggering of the closed-loop, message-response system, but in no way does that reduce the importance of it. In fact, the more effective the leveraging of the historical data, the more likely you are to have the best message-response you can get. But edge processing can provide the response quicker in most instances.

There are many use cases where this doesn't really matter. Turning the lights on, closing the garage door, checking the vending machine status are all examples where the latency of the system won't be impacted positively or negatively by moving the response closer to the point of ingestion. When the reaction time becomes more critical, say, in a car or any moving object responding to surrounding conditions, latency is extremely important. This is especially true in numerous industrial environments. Moreover, as we move forward, it is almost certain that certain systems in motion (again, like cars) will be interacting with other systems in motion (like other cars) where the broadcasting is proximity-based (mesh networking) and processing on the edge will be critical. Again, like most other elements, this is use case dependent.

Another key consideration is the local persisted store. The idea behind this is basic. If you are going to leverage the utility value of the data, you need to create a mechanism to do so. The local persisted store becomes the baseline for the data created by the IoT devices to be pushed to local consuming applications, as well as a variety of remote ones as well. There are a few important considerations here.

First, the ingest rate of the database must be able to keep up with the flow form the sensors. This isn't a huge challenge for most databases, but a consideration nonetheless. Second, ideally the database will make use of tight compression techniques to minimize the storage requirements. This is truer when the database is on premise on either a local server or as an extension to the gateway device, but keeping the hardware associated with remote processing, while balancing the need to reasonable data retention to a minimum is ideal, so the compression matters. Third, the data needs to be easy to traverse, meaning, if the database is highly tuned for a specific application, it may be poorly tuned for another, so the more basic maneuverability with respectable query performance over data supported by the database without undue administration, the better. Which leads to the last consideration, which is that the administrative overhead of the database should ideally be at or near zero. Local persisted databases that require ongoing administration could prove to be nightmare scenarios. This is an easy problem to solve. There are specialized databases that are ideally suited for these types of scenarios. The characteristics outlined here mirror those that have long been in place in the networking and telecommunications OSS (operational support systems) market for years.

An event-driven, publish, and subscribe architecture

While there are certainly nuances based on the variety of use cases and related considerations for IoT, most of these use cases will likely thrive best using an event-driven, publish, and subscribe architecture because of the nature how IoT messages are created. Specifically, a sensor-generated message tends to be an event, which is time-stamped, where the message reflects a condition or state at a specific time. The event might be the opening or closing of a door, or the temperature reading in a room at a given time. Once these messages are created, the associated record is seldom, if ever, changed. How the data is subsequently used can be in a variety of ways by a variety of constituents. Therefore, an architecture that contemplates a stream of events, where the creation of the data is abstracted from the consumption of the data lends itself exceptionally well to an event-driven, publish, and subscribe architecture.

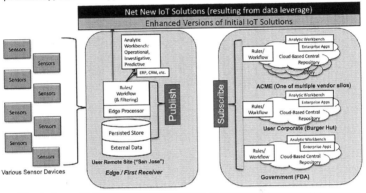

FIGURE 9.9: Publish/Subscribe Architecture for IoT

It actually applies in almost all cases for IoT, but how it looks may vary from use case to use case. At issue isn't so much the publish and subscribe nature of the architecture, but rather where it takes place. We will look shortly at the notion of the *first receiver*, which argues for the point of publish and subscribing to be as close to the creation of the data as possible. There are instances today where the architecture is entirely different, where the creation of the data and the consumption (application) of the data are directly tied, but it is unlikely that would remain the case for all but the most isolated cases, perhaps for extremely expensive and specialized systems for military uses or other somewhat one-off environments.

At the most basic level, an event-driven, publish, and

subscribe architecture anticipates the ingestion of records (or messages) as an event stream, although the stream can be packaged and batched in as well, upon which the ingested records are instantiated into a persisted store, whereby other users (ostensibly local or remote) can access all or portions of that information by subscribing to it. This concept is at the heart of the role of the *first receiver* and enables the effective leverage and propagation of IoT data thought the ecosystem.

The technology benefits of the right deployment architecture

From a basic technology perspective, there are many benefits for the right deployment architecture. This is true for the Internet of Things, but it's also been somewhat of a universal truth in technology. The IoT benefits are very similar, but the nature of IoT makes the scale of these benefits more of an imperative for getting this right.

Critical is the ability to adapt to change. We have all seen how technology evolves at an increasingly rapid pace. The sophistication of sensors go up. The cost comes down. The bandwidth of networks increase. The costs coms down. The power of computing increases. The costs come down. Locking into hardware, software, or sensors for too long can limit your options and drive up your costs. The right architecture should allow for component pieces of the architecture to upgraded or replaced. This is easier in some elements than others, but to the extent you can adapt, you win.

The right architecture can also help reduce the requirements for staffing and administration. For example, the idea behind the *first receiver* suggests a persisted store either physically or virtually at the edge. This doesn't mean a database administrator needs to be there to support these instances. There are database choices available that can be effectively either "established and forgotten," meaning, they have no real administrative requirements once established, or they can be easily remotely management with little effort or complexity.

Overall, less people should maintain the right architecture, not more. The best architectures are often the simplest and most straightforward. This does not suggest that they're not powerful or sophisticated. Rather, it suggests that the power and sophistication is delivered to users of the technology in easy to deploy and use fashion. There is massive elegance in simplicity. Apple has made billions of dollars by being extraordinary at this very basic concept.

Just as the wrong architecture can make servicing the platform and associated applications more difficult and costly, the right architecture can have a big impact on making the servicing of the environment less costly and more effective, especially over time. The right architecture should allow for troubleshooting and diagnostics on a component level, where finding issues, determining fixes, remediating the issues, and testing the results can be faster and more effective.

From a resource perspective beyond staffing, the right architecture can reduce, sometimes to a huge extent, the additional resources required. This mainly speaks to the hardware requirements and the network requirements. For instance, one arguing in favor of centralized computing might suggest it is more cost effective to simply have sensors paired with SIM cards and an IPv6 address, sending sensor messages into a machine cloud (in a monolithic architecture). Granted, removing all edge nodes and *first receiver* processing would reduce the specific cost of that hardware.

At the same time, depending on the use case (which is always your starting consideration), edge devices can reduce the costs of the sensor network behind the edge, based on removing the restriction for all devices to have SIM cards and carry an IPv6 protocol stack that require more power and computing resources than may otherwise be required.

Moreover, the sensor deployment flexibility associated with the existence of the edge device can also contribute to far less power requirements for the sensors as well. The edge filtering of the stream can dramatically (in orders of magnitude) reduce the stream volume, thereby having the same effect on reducing the network load (and associated costs) as well as increasing the value of the payload to the benefit of reduced computing required centrally. It is easy to see that the right architectural decisions can have profound impacts in terms of both costs to deploy and the overall effectiveness of the deployment.

The business benefits of the right deployment architecture

As important as it is to have the right architecture from a technology perspective, the driver for all of this in the first place is your business, however that is defined. The most elegant technology solution is meaningless if it does not help you advance the objectives of your organization, be it a restaurant, an oilrig, a hospital, or a city. The right architecture makes it easier for IoT systems to reach the right place in the right way and leverage the data needed for insight.

The common themes are around competitive advantages are to reduce costs, increase revenues, or expand market reach. In the context of government operations, it would be to reduce costs and/or extend the quality of life for individuals or organizations in the region, either through improved services or net new services. From an individual standpoint, it is either saving you money or increasing your productivity or quality of life.

Cost reduction is probably the primary driver of most IoT implementations today. By getting better granularity of your supply chain, you can reduce delivery times and cut fuel costs. By having safeguards against doors being left open, you can reduce energy loss as well as theft. By being able to predict maintenance needs ahead of time, downtime can be proactively scheduled, thereby saving millions of dollars associated with unplanned outages. Cities can reduce fuel costs. They can reduce the time and money spent on inspections, and do a better job at the same time. Smart appliances, learning thermostats, and smart HVAC units are working together to save you energy costs at home.

Increased revenues come in many forms, ranging from the changed business models of the product providers (think "lighting as a service"), to a better ability to optimize operations at a retail store, stadium, or restaurant drive increased sales of items or consumables based on conditional awareness. It may come in the form of increased services to allow more efficient traffic flows in cities both saving time and energy, but also allowing higher levels of productivity. From an individual standpoint, this could mean more efficient schedule management, more effective exercise routines, or better lifestyle decisions.

Expanded market penetration can come from a greater ability to deploy products and services into new environments with predictable and repeatable solutions that can still be centrally monitored and consistently deployed, yet also adaptable to local conditions. It can mean extending city services, such as increased public transportation or environmental monitoring.

The right architecture enables greater ability to understand and respond to conditions with far greater insight than before IoT. Specifically, with the right architecture this allows for the gathering, enriching, and subsequent publishing of the holistic data. In addition to subscribing entities being specific applications, the architecture should also provide for an analytic workbench of sorts, also subscribing to this data, offering operational analytics, investigative analytics, predictive analytics, and machine learning.

This starts with operational analytics for better situational understanding. Some would equate this to business intelligence, where there are key performance Indicators like a corporate management team at a retail chain might be using to monitor store operations. This could be something as basic as bar charts and graphs showing store sales by region, by hour or by product type. That graph might be capable of drilling down to further explore the granular data around time of day or zip codes or other dimensions that can be used for understanding what's happening at a given point in time. With IoT, the depth of available data goes to a different level. Instead of seeing store sales, you might be seeing which aisles are getting the most foot traffic or which shelves are fully stocked, or you might be seeing the relationship between store sales and inventory levels, or the relationship between store sales and vehicle traffic within a mile of the store. More than anything, you can monitor conditions at a very granular, thorough level.

This more granular signature gained with IoT can yield better insight as to cause and effect. Think of this as forensic analysis or investigative/exploratory analytics. This has largely become the role of the data scientists. Here the function is to mine the data to find relevant correlations and insight. Whereas the monitoring discussed above speaks to *what's happening*, this is more concerned with *why it's happening*. The data scientist might be trying to determine what triggers higher hamburger sales at one location and higher chicken sales at another. They might be further exploring why one-location ice cream sales periodically spike without an obvious driver. This is the beauty of the increase in data, where the ability to mine that data becomes a key to gaining additional insight.

Better operational monitoring and a better understanding about cause and effect paves the way for better lens into the future via predictive analytics. When BI tools are used as a lens into all this data, it allows a better understanding of what's going on, and the analytic tools allow for exploration of the data to determine why things are happening, then predictive analytics can form the basis of determine *what will happen*.

In the earlier (not earliest) days of IoT, product providers began to recognize that when the IoT-enabled their products, they could gather more data about their use and begin to model when the products would fail. This fed predictive maintenance capabilities, allowing them to proactively fix or replace products before they failed. In many ways, this becomes the embodiment of IoT, as people began to identify IoT with "smart products" that could "tell you" when they were about to break.

There is no doubt these capabilities are compelling. The wow factor of this new class of products is undeniable. A closer look at the possibilities, especially in the context of a well-considered architecture, reveals one last element of the analytic stack that offers a potential quantum leap.

Machine learning has been around for quite some time. Historically, the industry is rooted in "artificial intelligence." Although AI predates this by a few decades, in the mid to late eighties, there was quite a buzz around Kendell Square in Cambridge where several "expert system"[38] companies were based, but seemed to be akin to a technology looking for a problem. One of the discussions about how the technology was demonstrated discussed how the expert system could be fed a dinner menu and respond with the appropriate wine pairing, only to hear the response that "nobody needs a twenty-thousand-dollar machine to tell them what wine to drink with dinner."

While the industry seemed to fall from grace in the late eighties, the bedrock of AI moved forward, with everything from optical recognition systems to speech to text translation and other derivative applications. The notion of machine learning and deep learning has evolved from this, and projects like IBM Watson (and the widely publicized Watson appearance on *Jeopardy!*) are becoming well known examples of this. In fact, Watson has extended from the base offering to focused areas, including commerce, education, financial services, healthcare, marketing, supply chain, and especially IoT.

The world of Big Data that began coming into its own around 2011 has escalated on the back of IoT. This is a world marked especially by the increasing role of data scientists. The idea of machine learning is fundamentally the ability to "teach" machines how to interpret data and respond. A machine can learn that a picture of you and your brother is actually you and your brother, then spot you and your brother in other pictures. They might also be able to learn that if there are twelve cars detected at a

---

38 https://en.wikipedia.org/wiki/Artificial_intelligence#History.

traffic light, where at least three of them are compact cars and it is currently raining and between 35 and 40 degrees outside temperature on a Tuesday morning between 7:33 and 7:45 AM, then there is a 90 percent probability that four of these cars will turn into the drive-thru at McDonald's on the right halfway down the next block and order four coffees, two Egg McMuffins and one egg and sausage burrito meal.

What does this mean? It means that with machine Learning, IoT can ultimately deliver adaptive systems. It's certainly good to be able have management and operations staff understand what's happening. It's great to be able to explore data for cause and effect. It is wonderful to be able to predict future circumstances based on better understanding of data. But the Holy Grail may well be adaptive systems that are capable of dynamically adjusting system behavior to changing conditions. This enables autonomous driving. This enables dynamic security systems. This enables healthcare delivery that automatically adjusts to conditions, even down to the pharmaceutical regimen. And this creates dynamic, self-correcting city infrastructure that form the basis of truly smart cities of the future that may be a reality sooner rather than later, but remain largely unimaginable to most today.

On a broader basic, the business benefits of the right architecture can be viewed as the rising tide that lifts all ships. With the right architecture, data is more effectively leveraged. The idea that if I use data, you cannot use that same data is debunked. Therefore, the re-use of the same data by multiple constituents increases the value of the data for all parties. Therefore, systems designed as isolated systems employing closed-loop, message-response architecture, are severely limited in their value. The benefits of greater leverage for the right constituent getting the right data at the right time is fundamental value of the *first receiver*.

Chapter 10

The Importance of the First Receiver and Edge Computing

At the heart of this book is the thesis that enterprise will increasingly, and appropriately, demand use and control of IoT data, but do so thoughtfully and to the benefit of all constituents, thereby allowing for maximum leverage of the IoT data. Central to this is the idea of the *first receiver*. Therefore, it is important to look at the critical role played by the *first receiver* in allowing the enterprise that uses various IoT subsystems to effectively leverage data, while providing all or portions of that data to external constituents as well, ranging from the IoT-enabled product providers to third part supply chain partners, other offices or functions within the enterprise itself, and various other relevant third parties.

Fundamentally, an event-driven, publish, and subscribe architecture, as we just discussed, is the most obvious architectural deployment choice for the *first receiver*. This assumes that edge (or fog) computing will become a mainstream consideration.

In the past few years, the default deployment model has been a monolithic architecture where the IPv6-based sensor sends a message into the machine cloud. More and more, this will be called into question, in part due to the exact governance and architectural reasons expressed above. Additionally, the notion of pushing every single message into a central repository will not always make sense, because in many instances, most of the messages (temperature readings, CO_2 readings, etc.) are individually inconsequential, and pushing every message into the cloud only costs more money and diminishes the payload. There are many other reasons why edge computing will become increasingly important, but in a nutshell, we will see this become a mainstream consideration.

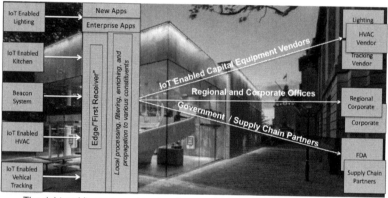

The right architecture provides local use and accommodates constituents

FIGURE 10.1: *First Receiver* Model

IoT is progressing faster than many could have imagined. As with any progression, the hype of the early stages usually gives way to a maturing view and market accommodation for the gaps that are exposed along the way. The Internet itself followed this progression. The early days hardly looked like it five and ten years later. Use cases evolved, the look and feel evolved, security evolved, and mostly for the better. The IoT is evolving now, and will take shape in many ways, but there are two noteworthy steps along the way beginning to happen from a mainstream perspective. The first is the importance (and leveraging) of data, and the second is the role of edge computing.

Organizations are beginning to better understand the importance of leveraging the data. Most of the early IoT systems were about alerts and triggers. You want to know when the machine stops working. You want to be notified the door was left open. That is all good. But many of the systems in production today don't make significant use of underlying data within a particular use case, much less between a variety of use cases, where the underlying data is abstracted from the use of that data. But that day is coming.

The stores that have beacon systems and lighting systems and HVAC systems and point of sale systems and other IoT systems will want to begin to leverage the data coming off these systems in the context of the other systems, as well as other operational data or external data. This should be obvious. For example, the time will come when the Subway store in Toronto on Yonge Street will adapt the lighting, crew schedules, in-store temperature, and inventory based on the known and predicted street traffic, weather conditions, sidewalk pedestrian traffic, prior sales (seasonally adjusted), equipment availability (and predicted availability), and perhaps a variety of other information.

Likewise, Subway Canada or Subway corporate can adjust their buying, scheduling, capital equipment purchases, and a multitude of other actions using the same information. And it only makes sense that the lighting vendors, the kitchen equipment vendors, and others also use the same information for building and servicing their products. It does not make sense, in any of these examples, to do otherwise. Leveraging the utility value of the data means abstracting the creation and ingestion of the messages coming off the sensors from the utilization of that data be it for ERP systems, capacity planning, CRM, operational analytics, Investigative analytics, predictive analytics, or any other consuming applications.

Edge computing is becoming mainstream as well. There are those who argue that the cost of communications has come down so much and the availability of resources in the cloud are so strong and affordable that it makes sense to give every sensor an IP address and push all the messages into a centralized cloud. It does not.

It makes sense to push some messages into the cloud. It makes sense, in some case, to push all messages into a cloud, but perhaps not always the same (central) cloud. Edge computing is the idea that you capture, initially process, and sometimes store the messages locally. This allows you to filter out the inconsequential messages (which may be 999 out of every 1000). This may have the added benefit of increasing the value of the payload of those messages that are forwarded along. It also allows you to deploy smaller and more simplistic (read "less energy and cost") sensors. It allows you to apply security at a local level. It allows for mesh computing, where low latency response to other signals in a certain proximity is important, like a moving automobile. Not all IoT use cases will employ edge computing, but many will. And not all edge computing will be physically local. Some may be virtual, and a cloud-based edge. But architecturally, edge computing makes a lot of sense.

Now let's think about why this is the case for smart homes. We all existed up until now with regular door locks and regular dishwashers. Over time, our more advanced capabilities might have been closed circuit cameras for security surveillance, perhaps a programmable thermostat, and power garage door openers with remote controls. But now that we have Bluetooth or NFC-enabled door locks that can be enabled or disabled for anyone's iPhone and learning thermostats and cameras that can be programmed to send alerts based on certain conditions, as well as energy management systems that link the thermostat to the appliances in the house, the HVAC and ceiling fans, and even to the weather forecast, and we realize that there is value in having these smart connected products work together as a product system. In other words, the whole is greater than the sum of the parts.

This does not mean that the participating companies supplying smart products lose the benefits they would otherwise see if they controlled the products. Phillips, Honeywell, Whirlpool, and many other participating suppliers will all be able to extract and leverage product use information like never before and shape their servicing and product direction based on much greater insight. Yet, that can be done while still allowing the user of these products to benefit from the integration.

A related concept is edge computing. Arguably, the central hub in a smart home is edge computing by anyone's definition. It is collecting the information from end-point sensors and triggering actions as needed. While some of those actions may be looped back from the specific product's suppliers cloud-based control capability, and others might be from within the edge computing (hub) itself, it's what we've begun characterizing as the "*first receiver*."

There are number of reasons why an IoT user would deploy edge processing. Probably the most obvious is to reduce the signal to noise ratio. A smart home in one thing, but a smart building is another. If you have 1000 rooms in a building and each room has temperature, occupancy, noise, CO2, and luminosity sensors taking measurements each second, then every message in and of itself is inconsequential. So, in a given day, of the 432 million sensor readings recorded, it is likely that a small fraction of those messages is used to take any action.

Even if you want to store historical data for richer analytics, it is still unlikely that there is a good case for keeping much of that data. Edge computing serves to reduce the "data exhaust" issue, which has the added benefit of reducing the network traffic in increasing the value of the payload that ultimately gets propagated beyond the edge itself. Other reasons for edge computing include decreasing response latency, increasing security (which has two sides of that specific argument), increasing configuration flexibility (as to the end-point devices behind the edge), and the ability to deal with governance issues.

When you connect the dots here in terms of the value of edge computing in some cases, and the user benefits derived from moving from smart connected products to product systems, and ultimately to a system of systems, it becomes clear that edge computing takes on greater value the more we move forward in time. The key driver will have less to do with data exhaust or even low latency responses, and more to do with the needs of users of these various IoT-enabled products, whether in a factory, a fast food restaurant, a hospital or something else, to leverage the entirety of the message flow from these systems to enhance their operation. Just like the need that exists in the smart home emerging today, the needs everywhere from the McDonald's to Mercy Hospital to Coca-Cola to universities, buildings, and even family farms will dictate the need for these systems to work together.

Understanding the critical role of *first receiver*

The role of the *first receiver* is first and foremost to allow for the effective leveraging of the utility value of the IoT data. At the center of this is the role of governance and data primacy. The *first receiver* assumes, but does not necessarily dictate, that the owner of the IoT data will be the enterprise that owns (or minimally controls) the IoT subsystems. Noting that a single record generated from a single sensor message can be utilized by a variety of constituents, internal or external, in a variety of different ways, the aim is to securely and cost-effectively provide a mechanism for allowing the right people/organizations to access and use the right data in the right place at the right time.

While the *first receiver* should also have several other functions associated with it (which we will explore shortly), the key is enabling the right architecture for leveraging the underlying data. A good example might be a fast food restaurant like McDonald's or Burger King or Subway. Let's assume you are the franchise owner of a location. Five years ago, your store had various kitchen equipment, an HVAC system, lighting, music, cash registers, freezers, security cameras, and other equipment used to run the store. This was the norm.

Four years ago, your HVAC system became a smart programmable HVAC system, and your lighting was programmable as well, with a "dashboard" of sorts on the unit. You liked this because it allowed you to pre-program certain configurations based on the time of day.

Two years ago, you put in a smart freezer System and smart fryer system, both of which would trigger alerts is there were issues with either, and both of which offer some level of control over these systems on your phone, over the Internet, regardless of whether you're there onsite or not. That felt really good. But it also got you thinking about the possibilities. You imagined your other assets being equally IoT-enabled, where you controlled your lighting, entertainment, security system, and all other important assets needed to run the store with your phone or computer. You realized you could maintain oversight as to how things were running even when you were on vacation. That was compelling.

Then it dawned on you. The information you got, and in large part, the alerting and triggering you could configure, while compelling, was a function of what the HVAC vendor, the lighting vendor, the kitchen equipment vendor, and all other vendors determined you could see (or not). This was your epiphany. You realized that there was value in seeing the operation of the various kitchen equipment in the context of the other equipment. You realized there was value in also seeing the information about the freezer and the shake machine as well.

The more you considered this, the more you realized that if the IoT data from all the products you purchased and operated to run the store could be viewed collectively, they could also be merged in with the point-of-sale data, the crews' scheduling system data, and the inventory system data to make better decisions on several levels. For instance, you could see cause and effect of changing the lighting. You could see patterns in the relationship between unplanned outages in certain kitchen equipment and sales from the point-of-sale system. You could correlate the people in line based on beacon data and what was being ordered and the sale data to the lighting, entertainment, and staffing at a given time.

Lastly, you began to understand that if the "signature" that could be derived from gathering and collectively understanding all of this IoT data being generated could be combined with enterprise systems like POS and crew scheduling and inventory, and by doing so, you could optimize your operations from how you run your equipment to how you schedule resources to what inventory you stock, then you could further enhance that signature by augmenting the data you are generating with your internal systems with data collected from external systems.

With that, you set out to import data from the city. A smart city project launched last year now generates data on pedestrian traffic, vehicle traffic, weather, luminosity, precipitation, air quality, and noise, all of which can be added to the "signature" you are creating locally, allowing you to optimize your operation and make more revenue while sending less on operations.

Enterprises of all kinds will figure this out and demand control of this data. But what happens to those IoT-enabled product providers and their ability to deliver the compelling features you like so much? If you strip control away, does it take away their ability to provide the enhanced products and services you want? It shouldn't, because you don't need strip anything away. This is where the *first receiver* comes in.

Again, the real key to the *first receiver* concept is providing the data primacy considerations allowing for contemplation of multiple applications across multiple constituencies to leverage the same underlying data. So using the same example, the constituencies are likely to be the restaurant chain's regional and corporate operations, as well as the potentially long list of IoT-enabled product providers (the one's that might conceivably be "stripped" of their capabilities by the *first receiver*), as well as relevant third parties like supply chain partners of regulatory monitoring and compliance bodies. These constituents can all be served, and in fact, can best be served, by having the *first receiver* that collects the IoT data manage the distribution of that data on an "as needed" basis. Therefore, in examining this, we would likely determine the following:

- The primary constituent is the local store operator. While the *first receiver* becomes the "publisher" of this IoT data, the local store apps ranging from the POS system to a management workbench are local "subscribers" of this data to enable or enhance these applications.

- The regional and corporate operations are "internal" remote constituents, who "subscribe" to this data, but in an aggregated form. The needs differ between the local store, the regional headquarters, and the corporate head-quarters, and the *first receiver* is capable of managing the propagation of the same underlying data in the formats and with the appropriate preprocessing as required at both remote levels.

- The IoT-enabled product vendors are also remote constituents. They will (likely) require the same data they would have been otherwise receiving before you introduced the notion of the *first receiver*. In most cases this will mean the vendor will get the information about the products they supply, but nothing else. The lighting vendor will get the lighting data, but not the HVAC data, etc. In fact, you want them to get this. The argument they may give at first for not wanting to relinquish control of this data will be primarily based on their understanding of their products and need to own and control that data to better support you and your use of these products. This is all true, and valid to the extent that they need the data. The notion of the *first receiver* provides they can get all that data, but it won't be at your expense. In fact, they would and should insist on contractual obligations on your part to provide them the data they need, and you should be happy to do that. The interesting side conversation here considers whether, under the *first receiver* model, you might be giving (or negotiating with) your vendor more information than you did before, or a preprocessed version of that information. For instance, if the formulas for eliminating data exhaust are mutually agreeable to both you and the product vendor, then they may want the filtered (lower volume) stream than the entirety of all atomic messages. They may also want enriched data. For instance, if you can provide them information about the operation of their product, but also correlate the information to internal and external temperature, that might be more valuable to them, and they might have interest in leveraging an enriched stream of data.

- Third party constituents, like supply chain partners, might want information on supply levels or kitchen equipment status to better understand the impact on delivery schedules and store needs. And while it is likely that some of the third-party data would likely be preprocessed and enriched data, it is to the benefit of parties to make that information available, but this, too, is enabled by the *first receiver* approach.

- Last, it is only a matter of time before government monitoring and oversight agencies recognize and act as to the growing presence of IoT and begin to automate compliance. For instance, the FDA might have certain standards about cycles on equipment or temperature for maintaining freezer items that could be automatically monitored via the same IoT-enabled equipment put in production for running your store. (As a side note, OSHA monitoring of industrial environment is almost certain to become a reality, as many top OSHA hazards are easily and cost-effectively monitored via IoT-enabled devices.

The relationship between a *first receiver* and edge computing

The early days of IoT were somewhat of a basic extension of M2M closed-loop, message-response systems, and deployed by linking the creation of the IoT data directly into a cloud offering of some sort. The market has steadily moved towards an understanding that edge computing can be effective in preprocessing the IoT data to filter, aggregate, and sometimes even enrich the data locally before it's propagated into the machine cloud.

By doing this, the value of the payload going into the cloud is increased and the cost and resource burden is reduced. Moreover, the edge can play a key role in both enhancing security as well as providing greater flexibility as to the sensor topology behind the edge, which can also increase effectiveness while reducing cost. That said, the edge is a subset of the *first receiver*, and doesn't generally persist the data or provide for the data primacy considerations at the heart of the *first receiver*, among other capabilities.

Moreover, the relationship between the edge and *first receiver* can exist architecturally in multiple ways. In most instances, an edge device is physical, located in the proximity of the sensors behind it, and performs the basic edge functions as described above. The *first receiver* can exist as an augmented version of the edge device, literally in the same physical instance, namely, a bigger server. However, there is nothing about the definition of the *first receiver* that requires it coexist in the same server, and in fact, can either sit in the server behind one or multiple edge devices and exist either physically in close proximity of the edge device(s) or exist virtually within a distributed cloud architecture.

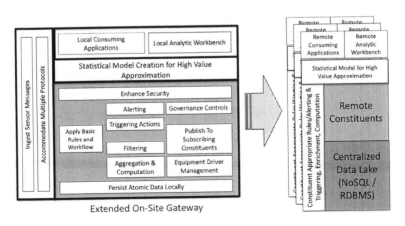

FIGURE 10.2: *First Receiver* Elements

Before we examine the component functions of the *first receiver*, we should start with the component functions of the typical edge device:

- **Allowing for configurability of the sensors behind it.** There is a great book by Francis daCosta (*Rethinking the IoT*) that makes a good case for edge processing. One of the more nuanced elements is the notion of configurability. Specifically, the idea that every sensor needs to be IPv6-addressable has real issues. For one, many don't need their own IPv6 address, but can sit behind a specific address (like an edge device). Second, the energy, memory, and related compute power required for an IPv6 protocol is overkill for many sensors and associated use cases. By configuring the devices behind the edge, the sensors themselves can be smaller, simpler, and cheaper. Mostly, they can be appropriate for the use case for which they are being deployed.

- **IoT message ingest.** The edge processor will receive the messages coming from the IoT devices into a temporary processing environment for analysis and forwarding.

- **Protocol translation.** There is a broad list of edge processors in the market that provide various protocol translation. Deployed IoT and M2M devices come in a wide variety of protocols and connectivity options. These may be very low-level protocols on simple, unsophisticated sensors, or they may much heavier, complete protocols like web services. To translate messages coming from one or more end-points into a usable format for local or corporate utilization, the messages being ingested in their native form must be translated into a form understandable by the consuming application or hub service. The edge device is an ideal point to perform this translation.

- **Message filtering.** This is a very important, yet fundamentally basic feature. Filtering for IoT message streams removes what are deemed inconsequential messages from the stream. For instance, a computational filter might look at the temperature sensor message to determine if the temperature had changed by more than 0.1 degree Fahrenheit. As long as the reading wasn't greater than 0.1-degree difference from the prior reading, the message would be deleted. As you might imagine, there are all kinds of filtering, some more sophisticated than others, that exist in an IoT world. But it makes no sense to capture, store, and propagate inconsequential messages, so filtering plays a crucial role in keeping IoT systems accessible and affordable.

- **Basic rules or workflow processing**. The early IoT subsystems, and really, the predecessor M2M systems, are best known for rules or workflow processing and alerting and triggering (which go hand in hand). The rules engine, or slightly more sophisticated workflow processing applies logic to the message stream. For instance, the temperature reading we just discussed might be associated with a low-volume fryer at a fast food restaurant. If the temperature of the unit moves above a certain point, it may require action by the staff or the vendor. So, for example, if it runs 1 to 15 degrees above a certain tolerance, it may write a record to the cautionary file to record out of tolerance readings, and it may also turn on light to indicate an out of tolerance position. However, if the temperature gets to 16 degrees or higher, it may signal an audible tone, as well as alert the vendor support desk that there is a "level 2-trouble" indicator at a specific location, where the vendor may elect to reach out to proactively support the customer.

- **Alerting and triggering.** The downstream processes associated with most rules or workflow is the alerting and triggering. Alerting is exactly what you would expect, some form of alert to a given condition. The light on the screen or on the unit itself provides some sort of visual or audible (or other sensory alerts, like haptics on an iWatch) that warns of a specific condition. Triggering is the actual action that is programmed to take place under a given condition. For example, the fryer reached 16 degrees over tolerance, so it initiates an automatic controlled shut down. Another example might be a video surveillance camera detects activity in a certain area in which a person is identified without beacon recognition as an authorized person for that area, so the doors are automatically locked and the video stream begins to record footage. This isn't new technology, per se, but its application in the context of IoT offers an increasing range of capabilities. This will come a long way very quickly, as machine learning begins to play a bigger and bigger part, but we can address that later.

- **Computation and aggregation.** An edge device, in many cases, will also be performing more sophisticated computation and aggregation. Reasons for this are broad, but for practical purposes can boil down to insight that can be derived from the edge stream than reasonably be processed close to the point of ingestion then propagated as imputed data (which is likely to be more effective and efficient), and messages that are most valuable to upstream constituents as aggregated values as opposed to atomic messages. An example of the former would be warning indicators that are a function of the correlation between multiple inputs. If part A on the fryer is running slightly warmer than average, but part B is showing a higher vibration level, then a warning is written to the operational hazard file and a warning light is triggered both locally and at the corporate operations center. However, if either condition exists without the other, then no warning is created and no action is taken. An example of the latter (aggregation) would be compiling the average temperatures for five-minute intervals throughout the day for a certain machine, where that interval average is deemed "good enough" for upstream analysis but reduces the network load and storage requirements and corresponding processing requirements by 95 percent.

- **Adding and enhancing security.** There are cases to be made on both sides (edge and monolithic cloud architectures) here. Some could effectively argue that whenever you open the connection or execute protocol translation you compromise the security of your network. The idea that all sensors are end-points for host-to-host communications likely increases the potential entry points and could also compromise the security of the network. Others would argue that "dumber" devices can also be less vulnerable, and in some cases, far less vulnerable. The thesis that more simplistic devices behind an edge can provide better security for the network also has merit. Again, the argument has merit on both sides, but most edge offerings in the market offer an additional layer of security, and the expectation is that this will become an increasingly important firewall between the IoT devices and corporate network.

- **(Limited) governance.** While we live in truly global society, we still must conform to many state regulations. How you keep data in the UK will be the same as in France or Brazil or the United States. There are certainly use cases where this won't matter, but if you are McDonald's, or the Gap, or GE, it will. There are many aspects to governance ranging from privacy to ownership to stewardship of the data. These considerations will be much more of a factor with a *first receiver*, but even without persisting the data locally, edge devices can still play a role in directing the outbound stream in accordance with limitations set forth within a governance framework.

The components and functions of the *first receiver*

The basic components of the *first receiver* include the expected functions of the edge as defined above, as well as the elements associated with persisting the data, providing for the firmware control of the IoT systems behind the *first receivers*, and the data governance associated with propagating the data to subscribers.

- **Providing a local persisted store.** One of the keys to the *first receiver* is the local persisted store. This is a database. There are several characteristics that are desirable for the *first receiver* database. Since the *first receiver* will either be an extension of the physical gateway device, or a separate physical or virtual instance, efficiency is important. Ideally the database will use as little hardware and storage as possible. This would also suggest the need for aggressive compression (10:1 or better) of the atomic data. It will also need to be capable of ingesting messages at the rate they are being generated (and it should be capable of significantly higher rates). It should be capable of operation without much (if any) administrative overhead. This is especially true because they will often be in remote locations where there is little to no IT support, much less database administrators. Last, it needs to be accessible via common toolsets. While the data store in the centralized corporate data lake might be Hadoop or Spark or other NoSQL variants, the *first receiver* will most likely be better served with a relational (SQL) database like Postgres, MySQL, or others. This allows for the entire ecosystem of business intelligence, visualization, performance management, and other tools to be easily used to interact with the *first receiver*.

- **Advanced governance and data propagation.** There needs to be the ability to establish the proper permissions so that the right data still flows to the right constituents. There are many governance tools in the market today that can accomplish this. These allow for the creation of policies to enforce which constituents can have access to specific information. This will include workflow, policy administration, and issue management. It may also be used to ensure data quality, as well as tracking data lineage, glossary management, master data management, and establishing and maintaining the associated business rules. In the case of the *first receiver*, the data maintained in the local persisted store will only be accessed and potentially cleansed, filtered, and enriched by whoever is responsible for the operation of the *first receiver*. The other constituents will normally be subscribers to all or part of that information, depending on their role and associated needs. The governance tools allow for maintaining the roles of engagement as to whom, when, and how that data can be accessed. It will also maintain audit logs, which are requirements in certain industries like finance and healthcare. This is also extremely important for ensuring the integrity and security of the environment. Also, most data governance tools will be capable of coexisting with related tools like data dictionary tools and data modeling tools. The propagation of the data will be accomplished through either function within the database itself or association ETL (extract, transform, and load) tools that push (or pull) the appropriate data from the *first receiver* to the subscribing entity

- **Equipment driver management.** One of the expected arguments against the *first receiver* is the imperative to maintain the firmware associated with the IoT-enabled devices. Specifically, a product provider may point out that "you don't want to be in the business of maintaining firmware," with the implication being the *first receiver* approach is unworkable because of the firmware. That would be both right and wrong. It is right to the extent that you don't want to be in the firmware business. It is wrong in that there is no reason the *first receiver* cannot provide for the maintainability of the firmware. We have been doing this with printer drivers for years. The *first receiver* must be capable of downloading and executing firmware updates in in the same way. The governance and security around this must also be managed accordingly, but again, this isn't a huge technological challenge.

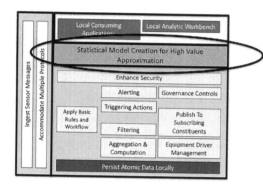

This builds models remotely then feeds centralized processing where data volumes will be extremely large and the ability to run high value approximation queries can massively increase productivity

FIGURE 10.3: Creation of Statistical Models

- **Creation of statistical abstraction models**. It is likely that most *first receiver* implementations won't include this when first deployed, if ever. But this is an elegant and powerful component of an IoT deployment architecture that can be particularly powerful when the data volumes and complexity scales to levels that become difficult to explore or gain insight due to limitations associated with scale. One approach to dealing with scale it to utilize sampling, where one might interrogate the data using only a 10 to 15 percent sample of the actual data with the assumption that the sample set is representative, and will produce a high value approximation. This approach has some clear and important limitations. First, if the use case relies on understanding outliers, like intrusion detection or network troubleshooting, then you potentially miss 85 to 90 percent of what you need by sampling. There are also significant limitations if you are joining multiple tables. If you join three tables, each sampled at 10 percent, then your effective sample rate is 10 percent x 10 percent x 10 percent, or 0.1 percent. The good news is that sampling will use the corresponding sample fraction of resources to run, so the resource cost is less and the performance is significantly faster. For these reasons, centralized machine clouds or data lakes may use this approach. However, assuming the concept of gaining insight through high value approximation is valid (and it will be in many cases), then another approach is to generate statistical models of the data at the point of ingestion. These models will be based on 100 percent introspection of the ingested data (running as an ingest agent on the *first receiver*), so outliers will never be missed. In fact, machine learning can be used as a part of the ingest agent to create probabilistic model associated with the message stream and flag outliers as they are received, then actually write an outlier file to be used specifically in user cases that benefit directly from that information. The statistical models, created at the edge, can then be propagated to remote constituents just like the atomic data. The actual size of the models will be 1 to 2 percent of the size of the atomic data, so depending on the needs of the remote constituents, be they internal to the organization or external, the statistical model might meet the upstream needs without requiring the atomic data. The model becomes the basis for creating a high value approximate query abstraction layer, where the same BI, visualization, and other tool sets can interact with the models, as if they were a normal relational database. In this regard, the abstraction layer becomes an extremely powerful tool for augmenting the centralized data lake. (It may be sufficient to replace parts, but it is much more likely to augment the operation to increase productivity). Unlike sampling, the reduction in resources is closer to 99 percent and the associated increase in performance can be hundreds or even thousands of times faster.

"What is the expected revenue loss from stores within 2 blocks of Burger Hut that have a drive-thru and more than 1200 cars/day where low volume fryers, walk-in-coolers expected to fail within 30 days?"

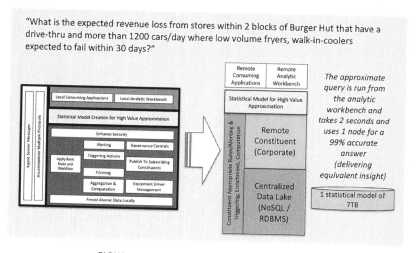

FIGURE 10.4: Approximate Query Example benefit

Example Query at Corporate: "What is the expected revenue loss from stores within 2 blocks of Burger Hut that have a drive-thru and more than 1200 cars/day where low volume fryers or walk-in-coolers expected to fail within 30 days?"

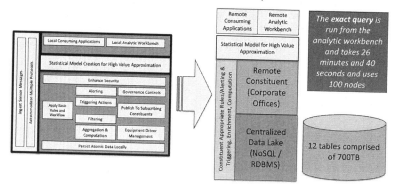

FIGURE 10.5: Approximate Query Example

Deployment options for the *first receiver*

It should be noted that an edge would seem to always be a physical, on-premises device. This isn't always going to be true. Figure 10.6 shows the reference architecture of a *first receiver* deployed on premises as an augmented edge device. The traditional edge functions and the *first receiver* are integrated into one physical unit.

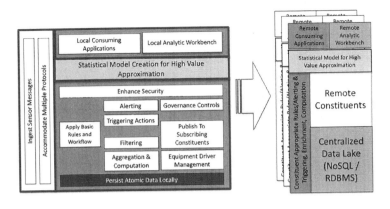

FIGURE 10.6: Elements of the *First Receiver*

It may not always be desirable, economically or architecturally, to deploy the *first receiver* physically integrated with the edge device. That isn't a limitation. Figure 10.7 shows the edge device and the *first receiver* decoupled into two separate units, but both still on premises. This might be the case for a larger operation, where the volume of data or the desired retention periods for local data is higher.

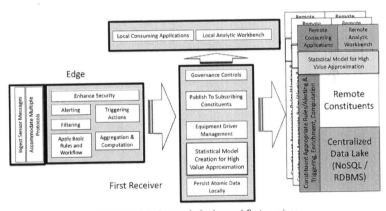

FIGURE 10.7: Decoupled edge and *first receiver*

Still, there is no imperative for the *first receiver* to be a physical, on-premises system. It can easily be an edge device connecting to a virtual *first receiver* in a distributed cloud. All the functions are basically the same, but now the *first receiver* is virtual.

Figure 10.8 shows multiple edge devices connected into a common *first receiver*. This could well be the architecture for an entity that has multiple similar edge operations (like fast food restaurants) where there could be rationale for consolidating several (like perhaps in a certain area code or region) in front of one consolidating *first receiver*. This could well be the architecture for an entity that has multiple similar edge operations (like fast food restaurants), where there could be rationale for consolidating several (like perhaps in a certain area code or region) in front of one consolidating *first receiver*.

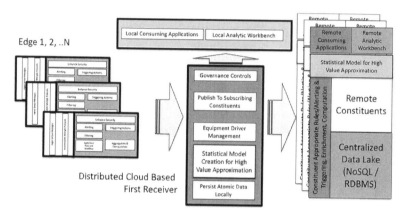

FIGURE 10.8: Multiple edge devices connecting to a cloud-based *first receiver*

In some instances then, edge might be in the cloud as well, and still not be the central processing point, but rather a distributed cloud functioning as the *first receiver*. This would not address all points above, but most. There is growing evidence that edge processing will become more and more important in the IoT. It's becoming clear that most industry analysts also see and agree with that trend. Yet, we are still evolving. As with most technological evolution, the market will ultimately drive the adaptation of the technology. In this case, the trajectory seems more and more obvious when you think about how people will ultimately derive value from these systems.

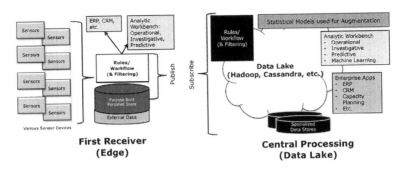

FIGURE 10.9: Event-driven, publish, and subscribe IoT architecture

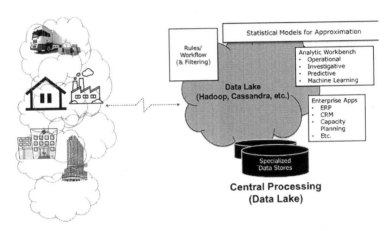

FIGURE 10.10: First Receivers tied to Centralized Data Lakes

Finally, the *first receiver* is most obvious in certain environments where there is a combination of multiple IoT subsystems and multiple entities that would and should benefit from access to and utilization of the data being created. This describes retail operators, especially larger chains including restaurants. It describes hospitals and especially alliances, where the alliance operates tens or hundreds of facilities. It describes many industrial operations, ranging from manufacturing operations, to oil and gas processing, and many other industries. It applies, but isn't likely to be as meaningful to certain consumer use cases, like wearables and smart home products, although even there the likely progression and maturity of the market will likely evolve along these lines, albeit on a more limited basis and likely through some type of iTunes-like interface for accessibility. It also isn't as likely to apply to instances where there are remote assets deployed via sensors connected to SIM cards with messages going directly to centralized machine clouds, like vending machines. But even in these instances, while there may not be edge devices deployed like you might see in a factory or a Wal-Mart, there will still be issues of data governance that might require *first receiver* capabilities resident at the receiving machine cloud.

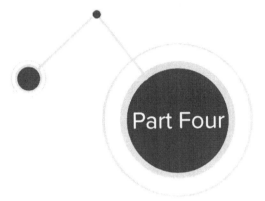

Part Four

From Enterprise Managers to Capital Equipment Suppliers, Entrepreneurs, and Investors: What This means for You

"Change is the law of life. And those who look only to the past or present are certain to miss the future."
–John F. Kennedy

Chapter 11

The Challenge of becoming a Data-Driven Organization

The next industrial revolution. A new technology wave. The transformation of organizations becoming data-driven. IoT is set to disrupt all industries and businesses by changing fundamental business processes through the use and analysis of data in real-time. And the benefits and opportunities of IoT and data-driven architectures are beginning to have considerable impacts on enterprises.

Early adopters are launching new services such as predictive maintenance, prescriptive healthcare, and fully-automated production processes based on machine learning and artificial intelligence. Entirely new businesses such as Airbnb and Uber have been created, leveraging data from multiple sources, and turning traditional business markets into newly, increasingly competitive markets on substantially different parameters.

Technology and business process challenges—around data privacy, data ownership, security, and governance—continue to pose barriers to the adoption of IoT and complete digital transformations, but there are also other reasons why enterprises remain cautious about the implementation of IoT and ultimately the *first receiver* approach. Understanding these issues is key to overcoming them. This chapter is about discussing and removing these barriers, and realizing the benefits and opportunities in the data-driven organization. These issues and barriers are illustrated in the following figure.

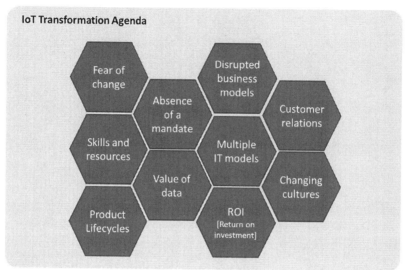

IoT Transformation Agenda

FIGURE 11.1: Issues and barriers in the IoT transformation path [Source: Emil Berthelsen, 2017]

Understanding the unknown and fear of change

Implementing IoT and becoming a data-driven business are completely new initiatives for most organizations. For many executives, acquaintance with IoT will have come either from networking channels, conferences, vendors, or articles recently read. The immediate association and "placement" of IoT within the agenda of the enterprise will be with information management and the CIO. In these scenarios, IoT is viewed as an extension of IT, and the enablement of another hardware and software solution.

Many cases and surveys suggest that a wider range of departments, including operations, sales and marketing, product management, support services, and finance, is driving other IoT initiatives. In these scenarios, department heads have identified benefits and opportunities from the data from connected devices. They have started to explore improvements to operational performance, customer experience, or new products and services from that data, and have started a journey of discovery not only in connecting new devices and getting data but how business processes and services are ultimately being transformed and changed with this data.

Before taking this leap into the unknown, many executives prefer to fully understand the implications and cost-benefits of such initiatives. This is where IoT and data-driven initiatives continue to face a challenge. The traditional IT business case is made substantially more complex by the very nature of the IoT solution being disruptive and requiring executives to explore, in significantly more detail, the opportunities in and value of the data. In many cases, executives need to think through existing business processes, and push the boundaries of innovation, which for many traditional businesses becomes an exceptionally daunting task. The weight of the status quo weighs heavily in most balances.

IoT and data-driven architectures require insights into both new and challenging business models and services, as well as managing the combination of historically distinct and siloed information management processes in operational and information technologies. To address these new requirements, executives will need to improve their understanding of IoT through the self-same sources that may have initially introduced IoT to the businesses, including industry analysts and service providers.

Despite this fear of change and the unknown, executives are beginning to realize the stakes involved in not exploring and understanding IoT. In a survey carried out by Machina Research in July 2016 with over 420 US enterprise decision-makers, 38 percent of respondents were already actively using IoT technologies, and a staggering 43 percent were planning to deploy IoT within the next two years.

Skills and resources

Understanding the complexity of IoT, and the launch of data-driven businesses, executives should be prepared to assess and evaluate the skills and competencies within the business to manage this process. IoT brings together and calls upon a wider range of business and technical skills, stretching from business analysts and business modelers, to IT and communications resources, covering the range of diverse and heterogeneous technologies brought together in IoT solutions.

As discussed earlier, IoT is significantly different from Operational Technology (OT) and Information Technology (IT), and brings together skills and competencies from both sides, and adds to the equation, additional skills in data management, business process reengineering, and ultimately, business transformation. Many organizations—running business-as-usual, while they try to identify extra resources to plan, manage, and run early stage IoT projects—will find supreme challenges. Increasingly, enterprises are having to partner and collaborate with service and solution providers to meet the architectural requirements of IoT.

Extended product lifecycle management

Smarter, connected products extend an extremely valuable and important attribute of their product, and its lifecycle management. Enterprises will be well experienced with the concept of product lifecycles and their management, yet with smarter connected products, manufacturers are suddenly able to extend this management and monitoring from point of design to the point of obsolescence. This differs significantly from previous lifecycle management models. Theoretically, the product was managed throughout its entire lifecycle however, "management" of products were highly constrained for OEMs when in possession of the owner, Here, the few instances of servicing and maintenance will have established the lifecycle management role of the manufacturer.

In IoT, and through the connected product, data as to performance, usage and condition of any given product is constantly captured and available for analysis. This allows, in those cases where the customer has agreed to the open flow of data from the product to the manufacturer, the manufacturer to monitor the product twenty-four hours a day, 365 days a year.

An enterprise's issue or challenge thus becomes one of managing this constant flow of data, and building the required business processes to provide an additional level of service to customers with smarter connected products. This also opens seemingly endless opportunities for the manufacturer to develop and improve the product for the customer, creating an altogether improved customer experience. Ultimately though, this means enterprises will need to think in new ways about its customers.

Absence of a mandate

Speaking to CIOs, the importance of a mandate from the business is crucial for IT transformation initiatives. IoT is no exception to this rule. Executives and heads of departments need to buy into the initiative jointly, and for a full end-to-end IoT implementation at scale to take place, IoT initiative owners will require such a mandate.

Issuing this sort of a mandate which secures the budgets and common commitment throughout the business tends to be preceded by an approved business case or ROI calculation. Irrespective of the mechanism, IoT initiative owners will need to be acutely aware of potential stakeholders and new ecosystems in IoT. How the new business models will work and where revenues will be generated from provides the greatest challenges in getting IoT off the ground.

Benefits of sharing data are slowly becoming recognized, as is the value of data that enterprises have been active in collecting and analyzing for business intelligence processes and for monitoring connected equipment. Generally, this data will have been collected through defined batch processes and analyzed using historical data analysis methods to support business decision-making processes.

In IoT, the nature and quality of real-time data has transformed the entire data scene. From historical data analysis, the focus is on real-time data processing and analysis, providing real-time actionable insights and enabling enterprises to achieve the operational improvements and new services as outlined earlier in the book. This shift in approach to real-time data remains well within the acceptable and "comfortable" boundaries of data management; only the speed and scale of data has changed. Ultimately, the end-use of the data for the benefit of the enterprise is traditional, and very much in line with closed-loop data systems.

A challenge appears, and begins to generate degrees of concern, with the entire concept of data sharing. Within the sciences and several international institutions, exchange of data has taken place for decades and decades, and within specific industries such as transportation (shipping, airlines, freight), extended levels of data sharing are recognized to benefit the entire industry, yet for most other industries, data sharing is still viewed as going against the grain of protecting your competitive advantage and sharing too many insights.

One of the more fundamental shifts in IoT and Big Data is the augmentation, aggregation and analysis of data, leveraging internal enterprise data, as well as external data from third party sources. These data sources may include proximity industries, environmental and locational data, and social data to name some examples. With improved analytical tools, the ability to process and derive additional value from aggregated data is beginning to show results. As this field of outcomes grows, more and more enterprises will not only be driven to share their data, but will also become dependent on other, external data sources for their own business processes. The shift to a collaborative data-sharing space is one that needs to be nurtured, and clear reciprocal relationships established, potentially within clearly-defined data communities.

Disrupted business models

One of the more significant transformations industries are experiencing from IoT is the change, or opportunity to explore new business models, either as a customer or as supplier. The sale of products has followed traditional business processes where the payment of product was clearly defined, as either an upfront commercial transaction (one-time payment), or in some cases, payment across multiple installments. This is to forget other innovative financial models, such as leasing, and refinements to installments models with zero or reduced interest rates. Fundamentally though, the sale of product was based on a fixed price. The utility value of the product was ultimately in the hands of the owner.

In these new models, payment isn't based on a fixed product price, but, for example, based on the extent to which the product is used, or what performance the product has delivered.

This thinking or aforementioned commercial models aren't new, and have been previously seen in everything from photocopiers charged per copies made to airplane engines no longer sold as intensive, fixed-capital equipment parts but paid in terms of horsepower usage. That said, IoT makes it possible to improve the accuracy and real-time aspect of the data for these pricing models. Engineers are no longer required to visit photocopiers to read the counters or inspect engines to determine the condition. All of this is remotely monitored and managed in as near real-time as possible, further enabling service providers to provide exceptional service and operational efficiency solutions to the equipment.

Such changes to business models stand to benefit not only customers who can pay-per-use rather than field the cost of having idle equipment stand by, but also enterprises and service providers willing to explore equipment-sharing models and more efficient equipment utilization. One such industry reaping the benefits is the agricultural industry, where connected, shared farming equipment benefits wider communities, although in some cases, the demand for the use of the machines has occasionally been at the same time!

Bringing together multiple IT and OT architectures

One more architecture. Another IT solution. Another OT challenge. Enterprise executives continue to interpret IoT solutions as part of the IT infrastructure, and on the surface, smarter, connected devices and specific applications do support this view. The challenge for enterprise executives is to identify the full set of opportunities and benefits from IoT and the data, and how IoT forms a new bridge between operational technologies (OT) and information technologies (IT), and delivers new business processes and services.

IoT isn't about adding another architecture to an expanding IT infrastructure. IoT delivers both an enablement platform for smarter, connected devices and as developed in this book, a *first receiver* approach which enables a clearer and more structured mechanism to manage data governance, security and privacy.

A new customer environment

A smarter, connected products provide greater degrees of insight into how customers use and manage their products, manufacturers are also able to better design and service these products, and ultimately provide the customers with new services and solutions that enhance the overall customer experience. Within the Industrial IoT context, predictive maintenance has become one example of this changing environment. Through the improved monitoring of machinery and equipment, and the improvements in analytical tools to make best use of the captured data, service providers are able to advance new maintenance services to avoid costly operational disruptions. In this environment, relations with customers moves from a highly responsive and reactive service to a significantly more proactive and strategic approach.

In this new customer environment, significantly more direct relations are established between manufacturers and their end customers. While many industries such as the automotive industry continues to be structured around dealerships, the emergence of the connected car and the data flowing from connected vehicles has also changed the relationship between automotive marques, dealerships and the end customer, and we expect significantly more changes to happen in these models in the future as for example car-sharing becomes an option.

Presenting the business case or a Return on investments

Far from a traditional business case, the IoT business case unlocks many new challenges and opportunities which need to be prioritized and managed in a roadmap approach. Compared to other IT and infrastructure investments, the initial development of an IoT platform should be viewed as a longer term and multi-purpose investment, enabling not just one IoT application but several during the lifecycle of the platform. Second, many of the immediate returns will be identified through the operational improvements and new service revenues generated, however, enterprises should also consider the potential value of the data captured as well as the potential costs and risks to existing markets should the company not engage in IoT.

One significant aspect of IoT is the competitive advantage gained within industries by first movers. Establishing key relations with customers as outlined above (longer product lifecycle management and a new customer environment) creates a longer-term relationship between provider and customer, making entry significantly more difficult for second stage entrants. IoT, like ecommerce, does not allow for a 'do nothing' option, and enterprises are well advised to begin their data-driven transformations sooner rather than later.

Also in terms of the business case, enterprises should explore how the ecosystem of beneficiaries develops, and as discussed earlier, should also explore in greater detail the possibilities of moving expenditures from costly upfront capital expenses to operating expenses through new models of Software and Platform as a Service models.

Learning curves for the organization

These are learning curves for the organization. In IoT, executives are beginning to understand the opportunities and challenges from IoT; executives are challenging their own fears of change, and looking closely at company culture. And most of all, executives are preparing their own organizations for the benefits of sharing data, the required skills and competencies of a data-driven business, and ultimately, having to manage and integrate different architectures.

The transformation process may be slow, and while IoT remains at a nascent change management stage, in terms of technology developments, the *'first receiver'* approach addresses and strengthens that balance between business and technology. Enterprises looking to leverage and unlock the true potential of IoT in the future should start with this build crucial and important building block.

There are ample challenges in technologically achieving smarter, connected products. Decisions around devices, networks, platforms and applications will need to be made as well as managing integration solutions and data challenges. Ultimately though, IoT enablement isn't just about the product. It is about enabling the entire organization to benefit from the technologies and the new business processes, and to achieve that, enterprise executives will need to overcome many of the issues and challenges outlined above.

Operational Optimization: IoT in the Enterprise

For years, operational systems have evolved by introducing more data to create greater insight and thus, more effective and efficient systems. The early manufacturing scheduling systems of the 1980s looked nothing like they did by the mid-nineties, thanks in part to data that could be converted into finer precision and better outcomes. One of the clear benefits of IoT will be bringing optimization to an entirely new level. Of course, this will take many different forms across a variety of industries. But regardless of industry, there is universal agreement across forecasts that IoT will make all industries more productive. The gains in productivity are projected to be in the trillions of dollars. At the heart of this gain is the ability to make better decisions and take better actions based on having a more granular signature about virtually everything.

With this in mind, it's helpful to understand how a more granular signature can be used in a variety of different settings, from use cases across commercial markets like retail, industrial, automotive, energy, and others to those in the public sector likes states, cities, military, and education to the consumer world of wearables, smart homes, and connected cars. The increased granularity of data offers ample opportunities, especially when that data can be combined and correlated with other data to improve understanding and achieve better outcomes.

Getting a more granular signature

While there are some schools of thought that suggest that too much data can, in fact, reduce the effectiveness of systems, the level of sophistication of systems today provides the ability to more effectively consume larger amounts of data and a wider variety of data that can collectively provide increased insight and understanding of many situations and inform actions resulting in better outcome. The fact of the matter is that there is more and more data.

Think back to how many of the IoT-enabled devices have evolved. Perhaps there was an injection-molding machine on a factory floor. In 1970 that machine would have had analog indicators about the state of the machine, perhaps showing machine temperature, gear speeds, or vibration levels. It's likely that a machine operator would record machine state in a logbook on an hourly or shift basis. The operations staff may alert the maintenance team if they suspected a problem. Seasoned operators were the ones who had been around these machines long enough to be able to listen to the machine running or put their hand on the side of the machine to feel the vibration and tell the maintenance team there was a bearing going bad. That was less a function of the readout of the dial, and more of the operator's ability to consume large amounts of data through neural processing in the human brain and determine a conclusion.

As factory floor automation became a reality, the world of M2M gave rise to the machine sensors conveying information to a central control module. This was the precursor to the IoT. With this came much more data, but it was still normally isolated to a single machine or silo. The sensors were fewer, and less sophisticated, but the predictive maintenance elements increased because there was still a much more granular signature of the machine. Another limitation was the connectivity. While there were more and more sensors on machines, not all those readings were available in any sort of timely fashion, and even those that were might have been subject to unreliable network connections.

The emerging world of the IoT is different. The sensors are both more widespread, by a great deal, and more sophisticated. The networks are more reliable. The growing ubiquitous nature of all assets having this type of capability creates a capability for leveraging massive amounts of data where there once was very little.

This brings us back to the operator listening to the machine and placing his hand on the side to feel the vibration. That operator may have arrived at that point after thirty years of experience with that machine. In the head of that operator were mountains of data points being processed to reach those conclusions. Today, we have the technology, especially with the combination of machine learning and massive amounts of data to automate the process that was engaged in the mind of the operator with thirty years of experience. We have the capabilities of converting that data into a very granular, sophisticated signature on which we can take action. While an amazingly simple concept, the implications are far reaching.

Using a more granular signature

A signature is derived for a reason: action. The early days of business intelligence were all about grids and graphs, operational reporting and KPIs. The idea was to use the data about the state of operations to understand its basic conditions. Was the factory running at capacity? How were sales in the Southeast? Was the load factor on the planes above the 82 percent threshold? This was (and is) information about state.

This isn't to lessen the importance of operational monitoring. It is both a basic, yet critical element of most organizations. Managers can look at the stores' sales and understand there is an issue with the Sandy Springs' store. They can see employee productivity in Cincinnati is off. They can see the healthcare business unit is 10 percent above all other units. The BI reporting, in and of itself, doesn't recommend any action, it simply reflects a state. The primary reason they're used is to allow management to draw their conclusions from the state of the operation to take actions based on their judgment. In this regard, the sales manager or production manager or flight operations manager is acting in much the same role as the machine operator on the plant floor listening to the machine or feeling the vibrations. At a very, very basic level, the data is being used to "convey state" to communicate the most basic signature.

However, there are more advanced ways of using this data. As we have seen, data scientists make a living dealing with mountains of data to gain insight into the knowledge within data. Hardcore data people are fond of saying, "The answer is in the data." This is generally true, but not always so easy to find. But data scientists are finding these answers, through both using statistical modeling of the data, as well as techniques for mining through the data. They are looking for higher-level trends or non-linear correlation that might be telling but not obvious. They find the "why" when they're seeing the "what."

That said, the two largest "consumers" of the more granular data are the predictive analytics and the machine-learning processes. Predictive analytics exists in so many use cases across a wide array of industries. Often the work of handwritten code by the statisticians or data scientists, the predictive maintenance algorithms use the signature derived from the data to gain insight as to the likely issues that need to be addressed with machines. This can be the light going off in your car, where a certain heat/vibration threshold suggests there is an engine problem that needs attention.

Machine learning not only uses the signature, but is constantly updating the signature to adapt to changing circumstances. In this regard, think of automation taking the place of machine operators who feels the vibrations, but then the same machine operator works on the same type of machine in a different, yet similar plant, where the vibrations happen quicker then the sound gets bad, in part due to different acoustic in the plant. The person, after some time, accounts for the difference in his assessment. The same is true for machine learning, where the interpretation of the data is highly contextual. Larger amounts of more granular data are the fuel that enable these increased machine learning capabilities.

Using it for business

There are a variety of domains where IoT exists, including personal/consumer use, governmental/citizen use, and commercial/business use. In some cases, these will overlap, especially over time. This section explores specific examples where the leverage of the data has a positive impact on business/commercial use cases. In these cases, the examples used are likely to be a fraction of the power and leverage from use cases in these areas a year or two years out, but they begin to paint the picture.

Retail

Not unlike healthcare, retail is an area where huge changes are coming. Ranging from innovative growth companies like Kairos to global giants like Accenture, there is a wealth of insight and innovation going into the retail space. The science of retail has evolved for both traditional retail as well as online commerce. At the same time, IoT in retail is significantly increasing the amount of data about the retail environment, to the point that this insight is leading to changes and optimizations for better customer experiences as well as more profitable operations. This means facial recognition detecting emotion. This means heat mapping to understand the flow of traffic. It means digital dressing rooms that "know" who you are, a good amount of your past preferences, the fact that if you leave the dressing room because you don't like what you tried on, you're unlikely to find something else and come back, so the recommendation engine kicks in and the store clerk is there with new, high probability offerings for you to try on without having to change again to go back out into the store. This is compelling, and requires a cultural shift to adapt to the new experience. Moreover, wholesale upgrading of retail infrastructure will take time, while this is a serious trend, and 2016 made this evident, widespread proliferation of this is still to come.

Industrial IoT

The Industrial IoT is one of the key areas where the most money and attention has been invested to date. This section explores a variety of IoT systems used in the industrial sector, arguably one of the more predominant areas of IoT, including how some of the key mega payers like GE and Hitachi and others are approaching IoT and the expected benefits in the industry world.

In the article about the importance of data and analytics in the context of manufacturing "Manufacturers Struggle to Turn Data into Insight," John Sobel, CEO of Sight Machine, makes a good point about the huge cost of getting things wrong in manufacturing, and the fact that not many other industries have more aggressive investments in analytics that the $11 trillion manufacturing sector.

Most agree the Internet of Things is the next big wave in technology, and by all accounts, it's a tidal wave. Recent reports show the hype around IoT has surpassed that of Big Data. To John's point, for the Industrial IoT—in which everyone from GE to Siemens to Cisco, PTC, Bosch, and others are investing huge resources—the capabilities being exploited today and the resulting insight will continue to develop and expend, especially in the context of the data.

This may be because of the legacy. Again, John rightly points out that automation on the factory floor has been around many, many years. Yet most of these systems are closed-loop silos, where the lifespan of the data is fundamentally limited, and the exposure to that data is limited as well. The promise of the Industrial IoT is rooted not only in the increased reach and sophistication of the sensor technology gathering this information, but in the architectural migration from closed-loop proprietary systems to more ubiquitous access to this information, both within and beyond the four walls of the manufacturing plant, or for that matter, the company itself.

To John's point, the benefits of getting this right, and the corresponding costs of getting it wrong, make a compelling argument for increased emphasis on leveraging the utility value of data. This is the universal maxim for the Internet of Things, be it applied to manufacturing, homes, cities, buildings, health, logistics, you name it. Assets that contribute data can also be consuming it. Along the way, data can be cleaned, enriched, combined, and leveraged to gain better insights, recognize the emergent patterns, and make better decisions and take better actions as a result. Said differently and in manufacturing parlance, leveraging the utility value of the data is becoming "Job 1."

Healthcare

There are a variety of IoT systems being used in healthcare including hospitals, clinics, and the extended delivery of healthcare via telehealth services and wearable devices. The market will surely contemplate the extremely important aspects of merging IoT data with other external related or seemingly unrelated data to create a more effective signature and the possibility for more effective actions and better outcomes.

The world of Fitbits and smart phone apps for health-related considerations are cute, fun, and potentially impactful to people's lives, at least to some extent. Many believe this. What's becoming much clearer is this isn't a fun little initiative where you can see how many stairs you climbed today, but a major force in changing the way healthcare is delivered (and empowered) on a global basis. This includes many elements. First, the extreme sophistication of certain wearable devices is creating digital health signatures in ways never contemplated (at scale) before. The result is an ability to do much more granular analysis—and at a lower cost. The more this accelerates, the better ideas iterate and the more we continue to accelerate, as new capabilities are built on the availability and combination of previous ones.

This dovetails into the world of telehealth. Arguably, this has been evolving for many years, but the increase in sophistication of Telehealth technology and the linkages with wearables creates a phenomenal new level of insight into patient care. Granted, the proliferation of wearables is still limited, but the capabilities of Telehealth are now much more widely understood. A doctor can do everything but touch the patient. The quality of the data being received and analyzed keeps getting better. The results are an increase in the quality of outcomes and a reduction in the cost of delivery. Think about this combination. The economic impact alone is massive, not to mention increased quality of life for so many people. No wonder this is picking up steam.

One example is heart monitoring that extends the reach and reduces the cost of monitoring in ways that would otherwise be prohibitive. Let's say you are having heart issues. One approach is to check into the hospital, hook you up, and monitor you for a few hours or a few days. This is very, very costly. More than that, in this scenario, you are evaluated under controlled conditions, hardly replicating real-life circumstances. The chief medical innovation officer of cardiac monitoring device company Preventice, Drew Palin, in 2015 said they can provide a chest-mounted heart monitor that you wear for an extended period. The monitor records data on an ongoing basis at a fairly granular level, along with other biometric data, synchronizing and sending that data to your physician via a Bluetooth link to your phone. The quality of the data injected under these circumstances is exceptionally rich and useful. The ability for the patient to engage in this "observation" is minimally intrusive, and the cost is so much lower than any sort of traditional in-house observation. The net result is higher quality healthcare provided at a much lower cost with far greater reach.

Insurance

Insurance, on an even broader scale, does IoT like the Oakland A's do recruiting. By now most of us have heard about usage-based auto insurance, where your driving habits are recorded for the insurance company, so you ostensibly get better rates for better driving behavior. This makes sense. The technology is available, via the OBD-II unit in our car (onboard diagnostics) and associated data logging to record driving behavior. (In fact, the early versions of this date back to 1968, when Volkswagen delivered the first primitive version of this.) Insurance companies have traditionally assessed risk on a sophisticated, yet still generic profile, for example, the likelihood that a twenty-eight-year-old male, living in Atlanta with a wife and no kids, with one prior speeding ticket three years ago, will be in an accident. Now they are enhancing it on how "David Palmer," fitting that profile, actually drives.

Makes sense? Of course it does, and with the Internet of Things, there is an increasing amount of data about how you live (wearables), and how you live inside your house (smart homes, security, energy, etc.). What we see for auto insurance is something we should expect to see for health insurance, homeowners' insurance, and certainly this will extend to businesses as well. This illustrates the utility value of IoT data. The data collected by the car isn't primarily used for insurance; the auto manufacturers for the servicing and product enhancement of their products use it. Your Fitbit isn't primarily an insurance tool; it's a health tool. Your IoT-enabled door locks, your Nest Thermostat and Big Ass Fan, your smart refrigerator, and your Dropcams aren't used for insurance, but the data can be. With that, the insurance industry effectively illustrates the big idea within IoT—the utility value of the data.

Energy

The buzz around IoT for the last few years seemed to focus more and more on the consumer side of things. From Fitbits to Fords, the dialogue around IoT has increasingly been about benefits to the individual. Somewhat less discussed, but no less poised to make an impact is smart energy delivery. Most equate smart energy delivery to smart meters. Again, this too, is consumer-focused. Smart meters are interesting, and play an important role. But having a smart meter embody the representation of a smart grid is like having the dashboard embody the representation of the car. Key to this discussion is the broader energy grid. For this discussion, we will focus on the electric grid, noting that a more holistic discussion will extend to all energy, not just electricity.

A smart grid is about balance. It is absolutely about efficiency. It is about dynamically adjusting and readjusting in optimal ways to deliver energy at the lowest cost, while delivering the highest quality of life possible.

The current power grid in the United States has been in place since the early to mid-1900s. It's old. It is also regarded to as the most "significant engineering achievement of the twentieth century" per the American Academy of Engineering. It is the largest interconnected machine on Earth with 9200 electric generating units, over a million megawatts of generating capacity, and over 300,000 miles of transmission lines, and, per the Department of Energy ("Smart Grid: An Introduction," as a basic primer on smart grids), is 99.7 percent reliable.

So if this trusted marvel of engineering is so good, why do we need a smart grid? There are a number of answers to that question. First, being good seldom insinuates that you can't be better, and in this case, a smart grid can be much better. Also, despite examples of ill-informed reporting, there are certainly limitations on most of the energy resources on Earth, and we are beginning to better understand this. As such, we are more efficiently utilizing the energy resources we consume, and are also beginning to incorporate ways to accommodate sustainable forms of energy into our lives. Smart grids can better accommodate these needs. Smart grids hold the promise of enabling greater comfort without requiring greater expense, at least long term.

A smart grid is an energy delivery system that moves from a centrally-controlled system, like we have today, to a more consumer-driven, iterative system relying on bi-directional communication to constantly adapt and tune the delivery of energy. By doing so, especially at granular levels, you can deliver greater amounts of energy at the right time and at the best price. A smart grid includes many components, especially the use of a broad range of sophisticated sensors (over twenty specific types of sensors utilized between the power generation unit and the meter into your residence) to constantly assess the state of the grid, the availability of power flowing into the grid, and the demand on the grid. It is also capable of collecting a vast amount of this information over time, using it to determine what "behaviors" can be changed to optimize energy delivery.

The most important concept in the delivery of electricity is peak demand. What that means, for example, is when it's really hot outside everyone runs their air conditioner. They also go to their refrigerator to grab a drink and then wash those dishes. And since it's so hot outside, they may as well get something done inside, why not throw a load of laundry in the washing machine and turn on the TV? All of this spikes the demand, and the utilities have a hard time keeping up, and sometimes they don't keep up. Even when they do, it's at a great cost.

Entire power plants are built to handle peak capacity. In fact, one approach that's been used for years is to build "pumped storage plants." That's utility parlance for a plant that pumps water up so they can run water down to spin a turbine that generates electricity. The laws of physics would suggest it takes more energy to pump water up than it generates on the way down. So why do it? The answer is that they pump the water up duing "off peak" hours, where there is excess electricity on the grid, and they run the turbines during peak load conditions to meet this excess demand.

A smart grid has the net effect of offering the consumer the ability to participate in the solution. In essence, we all "become the pumped storage plant" by agreeing to control mechanisms that run our dishwashers and laundry when the system demand is less, ostensibly in the middle of the night. It may also employ techniques to run the air conditioner at slightly reduced levels with great energy (and cost) savings. What it's also doing is holistically reaching to a very granular level to balance resources that previously have only been possible through central control with far less precision.

Making this possible are various component technologies that do everything from monitor the vibration on the transmission line to the meter going into your house. Phasor measurement Units (PMU's) are becoming the "health meter" for the grid, where the amount of information collected on the status of the grid will be close to 100 times denser than what's collected today. Just imagine seeing a picture with 100 times the clarity! And while the smart meter isn't the grid itself, it's certainly an important component. More and more, these meters are likely to be based on open standards internationally, and where consumers are integrated. This will allow problem detection more quickly and effectively. This will allow energy pricing to be based on the cost to deliver at a very granular level, offering a wider range of options on how and when we consume energy. Leveraging the underlying data collection for machine learning will enhance this. The more we "tell our household" what we want, the more those desires can be intelligently incorporated into the grid.

Using it for community

While many people associate the IoT with consumer devices, and the business world has been increasingly acclimated to IoT for improving business operations and even changing business models, the services delivered by our tax dollars are also being impacted in game-changing ways from small villages to large cities states and countries.

Cities

Today, the city without a smart initiative is a dinosaur. This does not mean all cities have reached the Promised Land, most haven't. But the direction is clear. These efforts include a wide variety of IoT systems being used and contemplated in smart city applications, including parking systems, smart utility delivery systems, lighting systems, transportation systems, environmental monitoring, and more, and the exceptional impact these systems can have on the operation and well-being of city and community operations. From Barcelona to Bristol, Singapore to Santander, Amsterdam to Chicago, Dubai, New York, Tokyo, Seattle, and all points in between, city after city is mobilizing. And it doesn't stop there. Smaller villages and larger states, national governments and military forces are moving towards IoT enablement.

Along the way, lessons are being learned. Unlike a manufacturing company or detail operation, a city often needs to answer to the citizens about how money is spent and the impact on life in the city. This means explanations and transparency are extremely important. The City of Chicago was an early and outspoken proponent of open data, and it makes a tremendous amount of data available to all through their open data portal.[39] There are nearly six hundred datasets available, ranging from crime data to budget data to data about taxi trips, housing, food inspections, and much, much more. While this is more aggressive than most cities are publishing today, it is a clear indication of the direction of most cities in the future.

The reach of smart city projects touches so many areas. At this point, there is a logical set of projects that fall into two basic categories. The first are the ones that come with a high return on investment, and the second are ones in cities that have established varying degrees of "smart city labs" for gaining experience with new smart city possibilities. Examples of the "higher ROI" type of projects would be the BigBelly dumpsters that "tell you" when they are full. These have been deployed in many cities, and

39 https://data.cityofchicago.org.

reduce operational costs be dramatically decreasing the required collection frequencies with the added benefit of increasing recycling behavior. In Brooklyn, Borough President Eric Adams said, "Smart city implementations such as these solar waste bins allow us to evaluate and monitor waste levels, as well as track data to make certain we are becoming more efficient in both our time and resources."[40]

Another example of high return projects is "smart parking." Smart parking includes on-street and off-street parking solutions and is primarily based on "smart meters" or sensors in the spaces that detect the presence of a car in the space. By having this granular signature, apps can show drivers where there are available spaces, eliminating wasted time driving around looking, as well as reducing traffic (often quite significantly) created by drivers looking for spaces. This also improves the efficiency of the utilization of parking spaces, allowing fewer spaces in a given area. The obvious artifacts of this are less fuel burned by the cars looking for spaces and better resulting air quality. The City of Westminster in the UK went live with Smart Parking's "SmartPark" solution. Kieran Fitsall, Westminster City Council's Head of Service Improvement and Transformation remarked, "What we've got now is an infrastructure in Westminster, which is providing accurate and good quality data and for us that is incredibly valuable information."[41]

In Schenectady, New York in 2016, they moved forward with a smart lighting initiative. The Wi-Fi-connected lights detect motion and can dim and brighten as cars drive by, saving energy.[42] Many other cities are launching similar initiatives. In April 2016 in Chicago, efforts began for a city streetlight modernization program. The intent is to replace 85 percent of its public

40 http://bigbelly.com/downtown-brooklyn-partnership-and-council-member-cumbo-announce-expansion-of-smart-waste-and-recycling-system/.
41 http://www.smartparking.com/keep-up-to-date/press-releases/smart-parking-in-the-city-of-westminster.
42 http://www.bizjournals.com/albany/news/2016/05/26/schenectady-gets-1-million-for-its-smart-city.html.

outdoor lights with whiter LED models, upgrading roughly 348,500 of the Windy City's street, alley, and park lights.

Since LEDs consume a fraction of the electricity used by high-pressure sodium lights currently in place, Chicago planned to fund the program with the projected savings expected to come from the higher efficiency units. The new bulbs will also last three times longer, leading to greater savings over time.[43] As has been seen with many IoT initiatives, progress can often be in the eye of the beholder, and when the IoT projects are government-based, the issues associated with them may not always be dispatched as easily as being overruled by executive management for commercial IoT projects. For instance, when the city submitted this project for comment from the citizens of Chicago, a group of Amundsen High School students called the project "terrible," after checking out the pilot lights put up near their school. A group from the school had been studying light pollution, and met with members of the Chicago Infrastructure Trust, which is overseeing the Smart Lighting Project, to argue against the LEDs.[44] This doesn't mean the death of this or many other smart city projects, but it does point out a process that is a meaningful consideration.

Not far from the Amundsen School is another smart cities' project based at Argonne National Labs called the Array of Things. This is a joint effort between Argonne (US Department of Energy) and the University of Chicago. The website for the Array of Things defines this as "an urban sensing project, a network of interactive, modular sensor boxes that will be installed around Chicago to collect real-time data on the city's environment, infrastructure, and activity for research and public use. AoT will essentially serve as a "fitness tracker" for the city, measuring factors that impact livability in Chicago such as climate, air quality, and noise. The goals set forth are to provide "an urban-scale instrument" that will enable the City, urban

43 http://chicago.curbed.com/2016/4/18/11450378/chicago-street-light-project.
44 https://www.dnainfo.com/chicago/20161222/north-park/citys-new-led-streetlights-get-failing-grade-student-led-study.

planners, residents, and researchers to detect trends and changes over time. Ultimately, the goal is to measure the city in sufficient detail to provide data to help engineers, scientists, policymakers, and residents work together to make Chicago and other cities healthier, more livable and more efficient.[45]

Other cities have launched initiatives to test IoT on a broad scale. One that's been around for quite a while is the Smart Amsterdam City Project. This initiative is broken into themes, including: Infrastructure and Technology; Energy, Water & Waste; Mobility; Circular City; Government & Education; and Citizens & Living. As of the writing of this book, there are 153 projects underneath the umbrella of Amsterdam Smart City.

In India, there is a project conducted by the Indian Ministry of Urban Development called the "Smart Cities Mission." This began with a "Smart Cities Challenge" where twenty cities were selected from ninety-seven competing cities for funding initial projects. The plan has been for forty more in the second phase and forty more afterward in the third phase.[46] One of the notable aspects of this initiative is the widespread participation of the citizens in the projects. The ultimate expectation is to see significant benefits creating a world-class infrastructure, sustainable public transportation, and affordable housing for the citizens of India.

Schools

While many people respond to the notion of smart cities, less are inclined to identify with smart schools (irony notwithstanding). However, those closer to the academic world may see it differently. A survey from Extreme Networks notes that the scope of smart schools extends beyond traditional interactive classroom technologies and can include wearables, sensors located throughout classrooms, eBooks and tablets, collaborative classrooms, smart

---

45 https://arrayofthings.github.io/faq.html.
46 http://smartcities.gov.in/writereaddata/newsClip/Smarter_by_day.pdf.

lighting, and HVAC.[47] The technology elements that come into play range from facial recognition to 3-D printing, smart parking, wearable beacons, occupancy sensors, smart lighting, and a number of other tools aimed at increasing student engagement as well as better tailoring education delivery on a more personal basis.

Smart, connected buildings

The benefits of smart, connected buildings reach businesses, cities, and individuals. At the core of the idea of a smart, connected building is a more livable, more productive, and more efficient environment. This can mean many things ranging from smart lighting to smart HVAC to better security to smart asset scheduling (like conference rooms or AV equipment), and much more. The idea of the *first receiver* is well highlighted here. Let's start with a building management company that owns and/or operates 500 buildings located in fifty cities around the world. On average, each city has ten buildings. Let's also say on average each building has twenty floors, and each floor has fifty rooms. This means each building, on average, has 1000 rooms. Without discussing the bathrooms, hallways, parking areas, or other elements of the building, simply looking at the 1000 rooms is an interesting investigation.

If each room has a sensor detecting noise, luminosity, occupancy, radon, carbon dioxide, humidity, and temperature, and each reading occurs once a second, then the number of messages recorded each day for a given building is 604 million. And this is just for the rooms. To assess and adapt to the "health" of the building, it is important to factor these and other variables (like capacity on the entire building, external temperature, time of day, and other information) in the context of all these variables. But if the HVAC messages go to the HVAC vendor, and the lighting messages to the lighting vendor and so on, then the ability to

---

47 The Internet of Things smart school is coming, LAURA DEVANEY, DIRECTOR OF NEWS, @ESN_LAURA, April 13th, 2016.

monitor and manage the health of the building is compromised.

Moreover, the value of a given individual message is a function of the outcomes desired, and not all messages are consequential. For instance, the temperature readings may only be relevant when they shift by more than .25 a degree. But that may not happen very often, any more than the state of the radon and carbon dioxide detection changes. The ration of inconsequential to consequential messages may likely be 99:1 or greater. This also makes a great case for edge processing (and a function of the *first receiver*).

If you happen to be at the corporate headquarters for the building management company, then your interest may be in looking at which buildings are "good performers" in terms of the energy utilization/efficiency, surveyed productivity of the occupants, and the revenues generated by the building, and which ones are the "poor performers." The signature created by all this data can paint the picture of what works and what doesn't. And the use of machine learning can "tell" the buildings what "to do" to be "good," like when to activate the air conditioning, change the lighting, increase the water flow to the sinks, etc. The answer is usually in the data, but the key is being able to understand and act on this data.

Military uses for IoT

As with many technologies, the military is fertile ground for IoT. For one, asset tracking is a key use case in the military, and clearly has been an early use of IoT in the commercial (and now consumer) world as well. This isn't just limited to tracking, but more holistic command and control. Another use is situational awareness.

In non-military terms, this is certainly applicable in public safety, it is equally relevant in military operations up to and including battlefield execution (from global, to company, platoon and squad commanders down to single soldier's level) including monitoring, sensing, threat identification (e.g. sniper), target positioning, marking, vehicles and soldiers status monitoring, environmental monitoring.[48] Also, just as IoT is having a big impact in the world of healthcare, it is being used similarly for military medical care, especially in the area of battlefield health monitoring.

Associated technologies for IoT in military use encompass the range of technologies in place for non-military uses, although there are certain types of IoT uses, such as hardened assets and military grade drones that may not currently be practical or accessible or affordable for the average person or company, but like many other technologies, will come down in price and become more practical for a wide range of uses, as they're further used by the military.

Using it personally

Last, let's explore the data being created by personal devices and the possibility of the more granular signature and how the individual consumer benefits, as well as considerations about who else might use and want this data and related considerations.

Connected Cars

Sensors have been on cars since 1968, but the world of connected cars has advanced dramatically in recent years as we migrate towards a world of autonomous driving. This section will look at the basic additional data being collected and how that data is contributing in the massive changes in how we see cars today and in the future.

We have now all heard about the Google autonomous car project, Waymo. How practical is this today? What needs to happen to make this a reality?

The driverless car is based on utilization of a pretty large number of sensors working on combination with GPS and historical data to allow a car (or vehicle of some sort) to go from point A to point B by understanding where it is at all times, what

---

48 https://www.cso.nato.int/activity_meta.asp?act=8647.

is around it at all times, and how to best get from point A to point B in a safe and efficient manner. As of the end of 2016, the Google driverless car has clocked some 2,000,000 or so miles shuttling employees in California.

Cars are getting smarter and smarter. The most obvious examples are the information systems in many new cars today. This includes everything from trip computers to navigation systems (with increasingly fantastic maps) to on-board diagnostic systems that alert you about almost everything in the car, from faulty lights to tire pressure. We are now at the point where mom piles the kids into the SUV, starts the motor, and turns around and says "Folks, we're going to need to be here for just a minute. We've had an indicator light come on and we need engage manufacturer maintenance to check into this before we pull away from the garage. It shouldn't be but a few minutes and we'll be on our way." In other words, we're all becoming captains of our auto-planes.

But it gets better. The sensor technology gauging where the car is relative to other cars, objects, people, etc. is getting better and more prevalent as well. This mainly started as reverse indicators to keep you from backing into a tree. Now it's stopping your car from hitting the kid in the street or parallel parking for you. When your suspension adjusts for potholes, this saves money and discomfort. But where is this going, and will it really be practical?

For one thing, much of where it's going is possible, but not quite practical right now, like the driverless car. We don't all have them ... yet, but it's possible. Going back to the airplane example, planes transmit a signal letting other aircraft know about them. Could we do that with cars? Of course. It's being done already in a pilot program in Ann Arbor.

You have probably seen "smart traffic signs" that advise you of specific condition, up to and including your own speed. What if the signs could talk directly to the car? In other words, the car could receive additional information that would be processed on-board to enhance the route or other aspects of driving.

And is the parallel parking the height of compelling features for parking? Not really. When you (or your car) drive to your destination and your car drops you off and then parks itself— now there's a feature! It's possible. Now. Becoming practical is a function of much more widespread adoption of these technologies and a reduction in the price points so it becomes affordable for the mainstream. We'll come back to a few "roadblocks" in a minute. Let's look at a few more glimpses of where this is headed first.

The information system that is so sophisticated on the LCD panel will become the projected information on the windshield or window that provides not only information about your car, but about everything around you. The data collected (and it will be a ton of data) will be mined for historical analysis and predictive models, making virtually everything more efficient and effective. And the notion that your car can sense the things around it enough to drive from point A to Point B with an optimized route and free from accident isn't even the endpoint, however far-fetched that may sound. Depending on your route, your car might "link up" with other cars driving a similar route, then move in "flocks" close together and as one entity. This is extremely efficient in terms of getting from one point to the other, especially in the context of energy utilization.

So aside from the money associated with this type of instrumentation, and the infrastructure enhancements needed to fully accommodate this, what are the other concerns? First, what happens when the computer stops working? Crash? Maybe. What if the network signal fails and the GPS system stops working? Do you drive into the lake? That cuts into the experience now, doesn't it? Then there is the malicious side of society. Can a hacker hack into a car, or a traffic system? What happens when the whiz kid gets his Volt to transmit an emergency signal causing the other cars to get out of the way? These are real issues.

Security in the IoT is a big deal. Safeguarding systems, including cars, will be an imperative. But the argument that "it can't possibly be safe" is ridiculous. Planes are largely computerized and they are arguably far safer than cars. Computers don't get road rage or get behind the wheel after seven whiskey sours. Computers are as awake after six hours as they were at two. And a given computer can instantly absorb and leverage massive amounts of learning from past experience. That isn't so true for a 16-year-old. Computers do text, in a way, just not in a way that kills thousands of people each year based on the distraction. And furthermore, the car that drives itself doesn't care if the occupant is 92 years old, blind, or impaired in any other way. So aside from the practical implications of more efficient traffic patterns and better energy efficiency, quality of life for people can be enhance. Last, insurance companies, healthcare providers, and public safety organizations will all be positively affected by a reduction in accidents and related injuries and deaths. The implications are very, very far reaching. And because of this, it will happen, without question.

Wearables

The existence of wearable devices has gone from the exception to the rule with large parts of our population, as has the type and range of devices. By now, almost everyone seems to have a Fitbit, Apple Watch, Jawbone or some other type of health tracking device, mostly in the form of step counting and daily miles run or walked. These have evolved, and now most have programs on them to track workouts as well as biometric readings like pulse and even temperature. But wearables are going beyond that. As the idea of the watch and the wearable move together, we are now seeing a variety of apps for watches. These range from more enhanced workout applications to sleep tracking to things like payment processing, directions, hotel reservations and airline tickets and more. And as sophisticated as the watches are becoming, there are a variety of other wearables becoming more mainstream. For instance, there is clothing with embedded sensors that track body temperature and movement. There are shoes than track steps, impact, and stride. There are very sophisticated monitors for tracking cardiac patients, and blood glucose sensors used to remotely track glucose levels and work with wearable insulin pumps. There are socks worn by elderly patients to track when they are out of bed, and GPS devices to ensure patient care of many types, including early stage Alzheimer's.

The real key to wearables has evolves for isolated use cases to leveraging the information. For instance, the early Fitbit users were generally happy to see the steps per day, where that "knowledge" provided incentive for them to take more and more steps each day. This is the most basic of closed-loop feedback mechanisms. A slightly more advanced illustration are the ankle bracelets work by prisoners confined to homes, where the GPS device on their ankle alerts authorities if they leave a geo-fenced area (like the boundaries of their home). But like all of IoT, the real value will be increasingly seen by the data. This is already illustrated by applications that consume multiple data points about your health to create a more granular signature and associated recommendations. One of the most obvious examples is Apple Health. Due to the sheer firepower of Apple as a company, it isn't surprising that a multitude of health apps and connected health devices support integration into Apple Health. This helps you (and perhaps your doctor) create a much better picture as to what is working, or not working, and why. As we see this increase in popularity, we will see an increase in offerings for utilizing this data and providing lifestyle recommendations, in many case without human intervention, based on the more holistic analysis of the data.

Then consider three other types of data. First, a drastically more personal version of data about yourself that can be combined with the data form the apps and connected wearables. Second, additional personal data coming from your environment but beyond the wearables. And third, data coming from outside sources.

The much more personal data is referring to genomic mapping. What used to be impossible but became technological possible but altogether impractical (due to time and costs) is now becoming mainstream. A person can get a full genomic scan for under $1,000, and a partial scan for under $100. These prices will only continue to fall, and the ease of getting them will continue to get easier. So, think about what can be done when you map all of your activity and consumption and biometric data with your genomic information. The possibilities are huge.

The second set of data comes from the IoT-enabled world you create around yourself. When you travel in your car, you can record that you are driving, how fast you travel, how quick you stop, and even readings like your heart rate (or more) while you are driving. Soon most can also record how close you may have come to an accident. You can also see how much traffic you had to deal with on your journey. You can also capture the temperature of your house (or office), as well as the additional stimuli like the lighting, music, television or other things lie the air quality or humidity in your house, car, or office. This, too, creates a more granular signature that can be used to better understand cause and effect, and consumed by machine learning processing that can help you optimize your lifestyle.

Last, there is external data that can be consumed to augment your personal signature. This can be everything from weather data to outside air quality data near your location to demographic data and more. When we talk about wearables and you think a Fitbit tracking steps, it makes sense to think this through to where it is going. All this data can contribute to a clearer and clearer picture of who you are, and provide the basic information needed to assist you in optimizing your life to meet your goals, whatever those may be.

Connected homes

As one of the early and visible areas of IoT, smart homes, have been increasing in number and sophistication for some time now. Some are beginning to understand the importance of the type of data being collected and what can and should be done to more effectively leverage that data going forward. One example of this recognition is the smart home "hub wars," which in some ways are an early version of *first receiver* concepts, including the role of the industry consortiums involved with driving standards to enable coexistence.

The "hub wars" have been a function of the introduction of multiple IoT-enabled devices for a smart home that are designed, at least to some degree, in isolation.[49] The smart lighting system stands on its own. The smart dishwasher stands on its own. The smart door locks stand on their own. Same for the security camera, smoke sensors, door locks and window and door sensors, garage door sensors, entertainment systems, washer/dryers and more. But anyone stepping back quickly realizes the need for integration. At the most basic level, you probably don't want a multitude of communications protocols to support, so having a combination of Ethernet hard-wired communications with Wi-Fi, Bluetooth, Low-energy Bluetooth, Zigbee and others creates administrative and potentially cost issues. And while it is true that some of the gateway-turned-big devices can reconcile the communications protocols making it easier (and in some cases supporting multiple protocols with good reason), the key is to be using the best protocol for the use case, and not a one-off selection made in isolation. But the more practical implication of all these silos is the inability to manage one IoT system in the context of others. For instance, the thermostat and HVAC system and lighting systems and smart window blinds should all work together. In the parlance of the Heppleman-Porter article, this would correspond to "Product Systems," where related IoT systems are logically connected and share both data and administrative services and are more effective because of the integration. When Google purchased Nest Thermostats, one of the next

49 http://www.makeuseof.com/tag/battle-smart-home-hubs-whats-whats-coming/

moves they made was to acquire Big Ass Fans. Why? Because
the smart fans can participate in the heating and cooling of the
house, and it made sense to integrate smart fans into a home
comfort system, the key word being "system."

As the market began to mature a bit, it became more and
more obvious there was a need for the various products to
hang off some kind of master hub that managed the integration
between the products and offered a basic command and control
console. Some of the early entrants were the Staples Connect
Home Hub and the Lowes Iris Hub, along with several others
(Wink, Insteon, Revolv, etc.) that were all moderately priced
and moderately functional but usually simple for getting started.
The interface of choice was the smart phone, which, more than
anything else, simply let you control each system from one interface. The idea that the data coming from one system was altering
the behavior of the others was not a capability of the early hubs,
but was certainly the direction of the market.

The real battle of the hubs still includes a reasonably large
number of hubs, but the key players are Google (Home), Amazon
(Echo), Apple (Homekit), and Samsung (Smart Things). These
offerings (and others like them) are offering conditional capabilities, where scenarios can be framed and the data being ingested
from sensors on one system can be fed into other systems which
may respond accordingly. Said differently, a given product (like
a thermostat or security camera) may "publish" messages via the
control hub that are, in turn, "subscribed" by other products (like
fans and window blinds or door locks and other cameras) that
process the new messages and trigger actions based on those
messages. The home hub is a *first receiver*.

In fact, the illustration goes further. The main hub units
(like Google Home or Amazon Echo) have moved to a primary
interface of voice. The idea you must type into your smart
phone to interrogate or issue commands may have now come
and gone. Instead, you may simply be sitting on your den and
saying "Alexa, turn on after dinner time" causing the lighting,

entertainment system, heating system, and even the fireplace to all respond to a setting associated with "after dinner time." What makes this even more compelling is the machine learning utilized by these systems. We first became familiar with this through Apple's "Siri." This is now widely in use with Amazon (Alexa) and Google ("hey Google"). While some are more sophisticated than others, the idea that you walk into the kitchen and say "What is my schedule today" and get your specific schedule read to you, then your older son comes in, asks the same question, and gets his schedule (instead of yours) is a reality today.

> *Smart home devices are now starting to make serious penetration in the residential market, I think because of the personalization of the devices. Rather than something sterile, users are now getting things with personality.*
> *— Chad Curry*
> *Managing Director at National Association of REALTORS*

Last, the illustration is completed by the inclusion of external data. The operation of your IoT-enabled devices can be impacted by external data like weather forecasts. Your schedule can be adjusted based on traffic reports. Directionally, these systems become more efficient and effective by leveraging data across a broader range, creating a more granular signature, and acting on that signature with greater and greater ease, ultimately learning and adapting without human intervention.

The symbiotic relationship between IoT and enterprise systems

Unlike most traditional technology systems, the operational side of an organization drives IoT clearly reaching into and in many cases. Plant managers, Operating Room administrators, restaurant owners and others all play a key role in the adoption and use of these systems. But the data and capabilities created by these systems must coexist with IT organizations and Enterprise

Applications. For instance, the ERP system or the Point of Sale system or the Patient Management system all can and should benefit from the IoT systems (and data) in place. The thesis behind this is that the systems are only as powerful as the data within them, and when the Enterprise systems can be combined with IoT data, and vice versa, they both become more powerful.

Let's look at two related simple examples. The first will be the kitchen equipment at a fast food restaurant, and the second will be the Point-of-Sale system at the same establishment. The kitchen equipment, in isolation, can do certain things. The messages coming from the machine (let's say this is a low-fat fryer) are consumed by an application that monitors the state of the machine and signals alerts or kicks of triggers based on certain events, like overheating or the supply levels being too low. The messages are also consumed and stored in the predictive maintenance program that allows the system to look for certain conditions that, when combined with recorded use of the system and length of time between failures might indicate an upcoming issue and automatically schedule maintenance ahead of time. This all can happen in isolation.

Now let's look at the Point-of-Sale system. Like most others, this records what customers' order, when they order it, and what they pay. This also is set up to interact with the inventory system so that the POS system can trigger inventory alerts, up to and including the need to re-order certain items so the store does not deplete their inventory. This also feeds all the financial accounting systems, and the POS is the system of record for sales to customers. This also happens in isolation, with the obvious exception of the linkages mentioned. In this case, these types of systems have been in production for years.

But what happens when the POS system can interact with the kitchen equipment system? Adapting to a more granular signature can enhance the kitchen equipment system, so that the predictive maintenance can become adaptive using machine learning. Having the thresholds adapted to conditions as well can also enhance the kitchen equipment system. And mapping use to expected demand at the restaurant can enhance the kitchen equipment system. Adding the equipment utilization information to it for better-cost analysis and promotional planning can augment the POS system. For instance, the demand may be greater under certain known conditions for chicken sandwiches rather than burgers, and but the characteristics of low fat fryer utilization are also different. Knowing the combination of the "product demand" and the resources available (and configurable) can allow for the restaurant operator to make more chicken available at a lower cost for having been able to model scenarios for the most profitable results. Moreover, the ongoing analysis should allow for machine learning algorithms to model the data and "teach" the systems how to adapt to changing circumstances based on a myriad of analyzed dimensions.

The illustration becomes even stronger when you begin to look at the combination of multiple sources, such as the fryers, refrigerators, shake machines, and grills with the POS system as well as the inventory system and the crew scheduling system. The symbiotic relationship between the enterprise systems and the IoT-enabled equipment becomes more obvious (and powerful) as the participation grows. This is absolutely a function of leveraging the utility value of the underlying data.

Enhancing the signature with external data

In many ways, we discussed this above. If one believes that the rich signature created by IoT, and in particular, delivered best through an event-driven, publish and subscribe architecture utilizing the *first receiver*, then natural extension of such an architecture is the ability to enhance and enrich the signature with external data, be it operating data, demographic data, or third party data up to and including external IoT data.

While we will not belabor the point by re-hashing all the examples, it is noteworthy that almost every specific example also applies here, from the extended signature of the smart home to the extended signature of your wearables and your health to the operation of your car, the operation of your factory, the functioning of your city, state, school, store, or even the battle-field. The IoT-enabled systems create the opportunity for greater insight, but that data can be enhanced for even greater leverage through eternal data as well as other organizational data coming from traditional enterprise execution systems.

The yet-to-be-determined possibilities

When cell phone technology emerged, it changed the world as we know it. We went from a land-line based world, to one where people started acquiring "car phones," where the power source for the phone was the batter of your car, and the phone itself was permanently mounted in the car (albeit not integrated at all, other than the power source), to "cell phones." But the early cell phones were the "flip phones" or other pedestrian phones that did nothing more than function as a phone, or at best, one with rudimentary text capabilities. Yet the phones we have today will typically have between 30 and 150 apps running on it. Users spend more time on apps, by far, than talking on their phones.

It is highly likely that the Internet of Things will follow the same progression. As we go from the enterprise applications we know today to a world, where the IoT applications coexist with enterprise apps, which themselves are augmented by the IoT data, it stands to reason that this will open the door to a whole new realm of apps and use cases that we haven't even considered. The possibilities will be enormous.

Chapter 13

Products of the Future: IoT-enabled Subsystems and the Symbiotic Relationship with Customers

Customers' expectations are changing. The purchase of the family car includes expectations about connected entertainment, navigation, and safety systems. The purchase of fitness equipment such as wearables and rowing machines comes with expectations of linked mobile applications. Connected white goods, lighting systems, and entertainment systems in the home are also expected to be ready for mobile or voice-controlled applications. An enterprise customer has very similar expectations from new products, not unlike the evolution in smartphone markets.

Heavy production equipment on the shop-floor has either become even more connected through additional sensors, or through shop-floor-wide solutions, such as vision and sound solutions to enable data quicker and more extensive data sharing for such applications as predictive maintenance. Transportation modes, ranging from lorries, trains, ships, taxis, and motorcycles, are sold or retrofitted with connected solutions to improve fleet and freight management functions, or improve customer experiences. Equally important, buildings and venues are becoming connected with sensors, measuring all sorts of environmental data, and making use of the data for such applications as power management, occupancy, and movement detection, health and safety solutions, and helping to deliver a substantially improved customer experience at these locations.

For product manufacturers, the question of whether or not to connect their products will remain a complex set of factors, including the value add of additional functionality, costs, safety, and service opportunities that emerge from the connected product. Ultimately, product manufacturers will need to make their products more compelling, use the information better, build more services and nurture loyalty, and deliver, wherever possible, new and innovative business models to achieve (or maintain) improved profitability. Let's explore each of these developments.

Making products more compelling

The invention and launch of the television in 1937 brought exclamations of "What next?" Since those early days, television—and viewing—has developed through a series of changes, bringing more functionality to the actual apparatus and becoming an evermore-compelling product for viewers to enjoy. What is interesting is that television was a very early example of an electronic consumer product being sold together with services, although not produced and owned by the same manufacturer/producer. And in some ways, the quality and market of the TV was judged by its content.

In the Internet of Things, manufacturers are facing a very similar challenge where their products need to become evermore compelling, not just delivering functionality and performance but also starting to be judged more and more by the additional services than the product delivers to the customer. For the car manufacturer, the quality of brand and performance of the car continue as strong factors in any buying decision, yet with steady growth in appearances, questions about connected entertainment systems, safety systems and navigation do form part of the new consumer profile.

For the manufacturer of white goods, the quality and lifetime of such product remains a priority. At the same time, connected white goods are enabling a series of new business models and simplifying such processes as reorder points for washing powder, managing wash cycles from your mobile phone, or assisting the customer in using the most economical settings.

Even in such diverse industries as agriculture, construction, and utilities, core products such as irrigation systems, harvesters, diggers, transporters, loaders, and smart meters are all launched with real-time or close to real-time connectivity options. Sharing not only the monitoring and remote management and control functions as outlined in Chapter 2, the data from these systems has started to enable greater efficiencies and productivity from the equipment, as well as partial automation in many others.

Making products more compelling used to be a design, segment proposition, price packaging, or technology task for product managers and engineers. With IoT, making products more compelling includes the services that can be delivered as part of the solution. These become new challenges for product managers, product engineers, and CIOs. The manufacturing of products has moved from black and white image receivers to high-definition TV sets with 3-D options, surround sound, and the ability to choose your own movies as and when you want to see them. This combination of product and service will undoubtedly require product and service providers to be able to deliver both a connected and far more intelligent smarter product.

For customers, these additional connected services may not add value or make the products more compelling, given the concerns around data security and privacy. As always though, security and data privacy is a trade-off between convenience/perceived value and personal concern. Most of the time, this is a moving point. What's noticeable in almost all markets is that competition has started to view connected products as an integral part of the development of their businesses and products, and as a way to maintain a competitive advantage. Making products more compelling is no longer an option, it's a requirement, serving both the expectations of customers as well as the requirements of enterprises for business process improvements and creating more efficient manufacturing structures.

Using the information better

More data is generated and transmitted by sensors in real-time than ever before. With a *first receiver* solution in place, data is persisted and managed with enterprises in a more structured and efficient way, applying elements of edge analytics and fog computing, and opening the opportunities to gain further insights from data through aggregation and augmentation.

From the point of view of the enterprise, the *first receiver* solution becomes the core data management system to enable enterprises to assign publication and subscription rights to data generated from within the enterprise. This can either be data from existing legacy systems, or data from newly implemented products, service provider solutions, or sensors in general, and through the active management of the data across the *first receiver* solution, enterprises are, once again, positioned to manage that data proactively.

For manufacturers and service providers, the emergence of a *first receiver* adds an extra layer to the architecture of data transfer from the IoT systems on the client premise to either an installed platform or the cloud. It also means that manufacturers and service providers need to agree, in addition to other commercial agreements, their publication and subscription rights to the data of their systems managed across the enterprises' *first receiver* solution. The *first receiver* also adds an opportunity for manufacturer and service provider partnerships and collaborations to deliver enhanced value by aggregating and augmenting their data streams immediately at the *first receiver* level for enterprises.

Ultimately, what IoT has brought to the market is a higher focus and degree of value from IoT data and analytics. Enterprise and Industrial IoT in particular has moved on from device and connectivity management and implementations, nurturing applications and enablement platforms, and identifying value from data and analytics, or in other words, using the information better.

The question remains though, what can the information in various industries be used to improve or enhance, either directly explored by the enterprises or delivered directly by the service providers? The following details a far from exhaustive but illustrative overview:

IOT BENEFIT + OPPORTUNITY	DESCRIPTION	RESULTS
Power management	Based on power consumption models and tolerances, identify optimal power management modules through analytics and real-time supplies. Manufacturing, intelligent buildings, healthcare and construction are key segments.	Direct financial savings
Predictive maintenance	Based on machine performance and condition monitoring, identify predictive maintenance routines from advanced analytical tools. Manufacturing, agriculture and construction are key segments.	Optimal asset utilization
Security	Based on location and condition data, and track and trace capabilities, identify additional means for security enhancements. Retail, intelligent buildings and automotive are key segments.	Improved asset security
Insurance	Based on real-time data on usage and location, identify opportunities to improve insurance premiums. Automotive and connected homes are key segments.	Direct customer experience
New services and business models	Based on real-time data on location, usage, performance and remote control, identify new services and revenue streams for enterprises (such as pay as you go models). Manufacturing, transportation and healthcare are key segments	New revenue streams
Safety services	Based on real-time sensor data, identify environmental factors including fire, temperature, pressure, gasses, and sun as examples for health and safety monitors. Construction, manufacturing, and transportation are key segments.	Safety compliance
Personalized healthcare	Based on real-time management and analysis of personal health, identify prescriptive health solutions for the individual condition. Healthcare is the key segment.	Improved health outcomes

TABLE 13.1: Overview of IoT benefits and opportunities [Source: Machina Research, 2016]

Using information better includes leveraging both the internally-generated enterprise data from connected devices and legacy systems, as well as augmenting and aggregating the data at the *first receiver* layer with external data to achieve enhanced insights and analytical outcomes.

Service providers and enterprises are the earliest stages in identifying benefits and opportunities from the increasing amounts of available data from internal and external sources. IoT, in parallel with developments in Big Data, unlocks opportunities to combine and analyze even greater datasets for additional insights using new techniques in artificial intelligence, including machine learning and neural networks. From these new and deeper analytical tools, enterprises and service providers look to bring additional insights and value to the markets in the near future, working beyond efficiency, productivity, and automation achievements as shared in Chapter 2.

Building more services and nurturing customer loyalty

Product managers, product engineers, and CIOs face complex challenges and new opportunities with IoT. Making products more compelling and using the information better are key change areas, and a third one is building more services and nurturing customer loyalty.

Fully-connected devices provide manufacturers and service providers with the benefits and opportunities as listed in the previous section under Table 13.1: Overview of IoT benefits and opportunities [Source: Machina Research, 2016]12.1, enabling a series of services to be provided, based on permission to access the produced data through the *first receiver* solution. The story goes further, as these connected devices provide unique and continuous streams of product performance data, delivering substantial benefit to product engineers and designers. With real-time product feedback, product design processes and feedback loops are substantially shortened and improvements can be made immediately as and where required, as compared to waiting for lengthy product survey cycles or, at worst, failure rates.

This 24/7 continuous stream of real-time performance data and associated services opens a second and, perhaps, more significant challenge for product manufacturers, customer services, and extended product and customer lifecycles. As a product manufacturer, the main efforts were in the design, build, test, and launch of the product, with subsequent attention to the actual performance and quality of the product when in the customer's possession. Generally, once in the possession of the customer, well, that may be compared to the dark side of the moon. But the transformation to IoT-enabled products changes that equation.

In the age of connected devices, product manufacturers can monitor customer products constantly, and provide, where agreed, associated services and warranty management routines as required. It also obliges the product manufacturer, as compared to previously, to have a fully functional customer support service function with a continuous history of the product, including firmware updates and any issues previously addressed and resolved. In effect, the lifecycle of both the product and the customer have been extended; for some product manufacturers and CIOs, this is a real challenge, and for others, it's another set of opportunities for future services and engagements.

Delivering new and innovative business models to achieve improved profitability

Product managers and CIOs of product manufacturers need to work closely with the rest of the organization and explore how new and innovative business models can actually change the entire business and deliver new levels of improved profitability. In many of the value-added services identified in this report, OEMs are viewed as enhancing their company portfolios of products with new services such as predictive maintenance and improved servicing. These are logical extensions of the available data from the connected products, and definitely add to the value perceived and experienced by the customers. They generate new revenue streams with potentially greater profitability, as costs are directly impacted by the quality of the products and the predictive capabilities.

In addition to these immediate and "low-hanging fruit" services, OEMs should begin to explore more significant transformations to their industry and businesses. The concept of servitization has been previously addressed, and unlocks the opportunities for enterprises to evaluate existing and potential business models for their products and services, transforming not only engagement models with customers (through services) and potentially redesigning commercial models from CAPEX- to OPEX-based models, utilizing connected products to measure usage, and potentially selling services instead of products.

Examples of servitization approaches are becoming better known in different industries today. In heavy industry, machine equipment is being paid for in terms of output and pressure applied in, for example, die-casting. In the aviation industry, airplane manufacturers, in terms of engine horsepower used rather than a fixed subscription or leasing model, have for a longer time paid for airplane engines. And in the lighting industry, several traditional light bulb manufacturers have enhanced their lighting fixtures with connected sensors, and now provide a substantially wider range of services such as occupancy and security monitoring, as part of the solution rather than just selling light bulbs.

These have become significant transformations for the enterprise. This isn't just the digital transformation of the business and its processes but more fundamentally, a complete transformation of the products, services and ways of doing business for the enterprise and its people. For product managers, engineers and CIOs, these changes are just the start of a substantially richer and longer IoT journey, enabled by the *first receiver* solution.

The call for action for product managers, product engineers and CIOs

As written many places in this book, IoT is a disruptive market force. Through connected devices, products, and services, and enhanced capabilities in IoT data and analytics, industries are being transformed. Enterprises need to prepare and ultimately participate in these transformations to remain competitive. Product managers, product engineers, and CIOs and their IT departments are, in particular, on the frontline of all these changes.

Making products more compelling, using information better, building more services and nurturing customer loyalty, and delivering where possible new and innovative business models to achieve (or at least maintain) improved profitability are becoming some of the new priorities for these resources in the enterprise. For some, they will be prepared; for others, they are preparing themselves and beginning to explore the challenges and issues in IoT. It is for this latter group that this book has been written, and shares the importance of the *first receiver* approach as a learning lesson from many of the earlier implementations and trials in IoT. The call to action for product managers, product engineers, and CIOs and their IT departments: build and deploy the right architectures for IoT from the beginning.

Chapter 14

One + One = 2,000,000: The Combinatorial
Opportunities for Innovators and Entrepreneurs

Erik Brynjolfsson and Andrew McAfee in their book, *The Second Machine Age*, spoke of the exponential power of "combinatorial innovation," and in this concept resides one of the real strengths of the IoT: the availability and ability to combine different ideas, technologies, and applications to create new inventions and create value.

IoT is a journey of discovery and innovation, and several of the attributes of IoT, such as open source and standards, and associated terms, such as openness, flexibility, and agility all contribute to this process of continuous and contributive innovation. In fact, innovation needs to continue down the path of both proprietary solutions and of open solutions, sharing all sorts of things (data, ideas, codes, applications, and so on), building on them, and creating and producing new and innovative solutions. Ultimately, it is a question of creating value.

From combinatorial innovations, three distinct sets of values are identifiable: direct, associated, and societal values. Exploring the various combinatorial opportunities and financial impacts IoT has on enterprises is critical for chief innovation officers and heads of business strategy to understand and prepare for. The success of IoT and digital transformations rests on delivering and realizing these financial values.

Before we look at the specifics, one place to start may be with these questions: What does this IoT represent financially? Where is the financial burden or savings realized? Why? What has to happen for the savings and returns on investment of these systems? What assumptions are inherent to the financial projections regarding the IoT? These are questions being asked by more and more people and organizations.

Let's start with the basics. Will the IoT drive financial value? Yes. According to the recent Cisco study, there is $14.4 trillion of "value at stake" over the next decade. And while it's hard to guess how accurate this really is, the study is impressive. This figure is broken down further:

- Asset utilization ($2.5 trillion). IoE reduces selling, general, and administrative (SG&A) expenses and cost of goods sold (CoGS) by improving business process execution and capital efficiency.
- Employee productivity ($2.5 trillion). IoE creates labor efficiencies that result in fewer or more productive person-hours.
- Supply chain and logistics ($2.7 trillion). IoE eliminates waste and improves process efficiencies.
- Customer experience ($3.7 trillion). IoE increases customer lifetime value and grows market share by adding more customers.
- Innovation, including reducing time to market ($3.0 trillion). IoE increases the return on R&D investments, reduces time to market, and creates additional revenue streams from new business models and opportunities.

But what exactly is value? In a blog by Chris Rezendes, President of INEX Advisors, he spoke about the discussions he had with a number of people at the Cisco conference recently (where the study referenced here was introduced). According to Chris, the growing consensus was that "value" is best defined as a function of economic stability. So there are certainly elements of direct financial benefit, but the discussion extends beyond that. Can an energy company make more money by delivering energy more efficiently? Of course. Can a manufacturer make more money by further optimizing the supply chain? Again, yes—this is obvious. But what happens when people who are living in underdeveloped areas can see significant gains in quality of life?

One example Chris referenced was a person walking miles to find clean well water. If this information could be made available, it could potentially save vast amounts of time, allowing the person to, perhaps, even gain better employment. When quality of life—ranging from developing nations to smaller cities and depressed towns in the developed world that need redeveloping—is enhanced, then people's focus and energy can become even more effective and efficient. Employment, infrastructure, healthcare, and overall well-being should improve.

Intuitively, it is easy to conclude that the myriad of capabilities brought about by the IoT will yield value. When you spend less time in your car because of smart traffic systems, there is value. When time and costs associated with diagnosing medical conditions decrease, especially when it involves someone at a remote location, there is value. When your household energy consumption and corresponding appliance configurations respond to external conditions ranging from the weather to the load on the grid, there is value.

The Cisco study was interesting in that it made some very tangible assessments of this value. It pertained to the private sector, and the value will certainly extend far beyond. That said, the report by Cisco, as well as reports, comments, ideas, and other input from the likes of GE, McKinsey, Accenture, and many, many other organizations (including non-profit industry groups like the W3C) point to a connected world that economically, among other things, will be fundamentally changed.

The $14.4 trillion number is compelling for certain. The real value of the Internet of Things is likely to be measured in numbers far greater. There are many other considerations, including security and privacy that represent potential issues along the way. It is reasonably certain that the IoT is both here to stay, and valuable by anyone's definition.

Direct, tangible savings, and values from IoT

Four IoT applications lead the race for substantial economic value by 2025 according to the 2015 McKinsey Report.[50] In the settings of manufacturing and worksites, the three applications of operations optimization, predictive maintenance and improved equipment maintenance form the core of direct and tangible savings for enterprises. The fourth, in the setting called Outside, identifies logistics routing as the key application. Together, these four applications deliver close to 30 percent of the $11 trillion expected economic impact of IoT on the nine settings outlined. Those who continue their search for the killer app should take note of the size of these opportunities, and look to how significantly IoT will impact industries in these four process areas.

Within the settings of manufacturing and worksites, there are other applications, which directly contribute to the economic impacts from IoT. Inventory optimization, health and safety management, autonomous transport, and supply chain improvements and efficiency are additional opportunities. These are direct, tangible, and immediate savings that industrial enterprises can identify on their P&Ls and balance sheets. The opportunities continue to grow, and when one begins to look at aggregating and combining the data from the various data sources and applications, and potentially establishing fully-automated and integrated end-to-end business processes leveraging IoT, the size of the economic impact grows.

Additional direct and tangible benefits include improved sales revenue streams from retail analytics, direct power management savings from intelligent power solutions which avoid peak pricing, balancing demand with availability, and, in healthcare,

---

50 McKinsey Global Institute, "The Internet of Things: Mapping the Value of the Hype," June 2015.

reducing costs in several of the business processes including assisted living, connected medical environments, and clinical remote monitoring.

As M2M and IoT solutions continue to mature, augmented with the *first receiver* solution, enterprises improve their abilities to manage and generate additional value from applications as well as data. It's this interoperability of the applications and data, or the combinatorial opportunities which McKinsey has estimated delivers over $4 trillion of the estimated $11.1 trillion economic impact. To manage that interoperability, maintain data governance and privacy, and achieve the tangible economic opportunities of IoT, the importance of the *first receiver* solution becomes evermore critical for an enterprise to establish.

Associated, intangible values from IoT

The delivery of direct and tangible value from IoT applications and data remains the priority for chief innovation officers and heads of business strategy. These outcomes are what drives and further assists developments in IoT. However, chief innovation officers and heads of business strategy have also been key contributors to identifying associated, intangible values. Earlier, stability was raised as an important associated value from IoT. Others include infrastructure, sharing of information, improved productivity, and health and safety.

Most industry executives will agree that one of their key strengths is their employee base, and securing the well-being, health, and safety of staff should be one of the priorities of any company. Applications such as mining industry helmets with heat and sun sensors to avoid overheating, or gas sensors on wearables and uniforms are becoming commonplace, and delivering new and important innovations that ensure staff health and safety, ultimately supporting stability and economic growth.

One of the earliest adoption areas of IoT is in in-vehicle emergency call systems and roadside assistance. Measured in terms of direct and tangible value, these may be life-saving devices but also provide significant levels of safety for all drivers and road traffic in general.

Another advantage of IoT applications is the ability to help improve employee productivity. Through, for example, augmented reality and connected machinery with training guidelines, employees are able to address and resolve problems quicker, and, with continuous training, improve business processes. Everything from removing significant causes of lost time, locating items quicker, reducing excess waste and unnecessary stockpiles of materials are ways in which IoT applications are assisting overall business productivity.

IoT, with the *first receiver* solution, is an infrastructure where the sharing of data and information is enabled at the highest of levels. This infrastructure and the workings of IoT in general are what unlock the opportunities to aggregate and combine data, ideas, applications and at the practical level, coding and programs. In fact, combinatorial innovation is represented by the developments to date in M2M and IoT as discussed in Chapter 2, moving from monitoring, to remote management and control, to efficiency and productivity, and automation, and operational data spaces.

Ultimately, data sharing delivers a host of associated and intangible values which include greater efficiency by removing duplication, building on lessons learned, improving overall knowledge management, reduces risk, helps meet regulatory requirements and compliance goals, and improves delivery of existing and new services.

Societal values from IoT

Better health, education, welfare and security are four of the pillars which IoT begins to deliver to society. In the context of Smart Cities, public services are radically being enhanced and augmented with IoT led solutions such as Intelligent Transport Services, road planning and traffic monitoring, environmental monitoring and so on. Included here are such safety features as

CCTV and security solutions, and improvements to all emergency services in either the planning, execution or preparations for their services.

In terms of education, it isn't only the training of employees but of anyone through the new techniques and tools available through IoT including for medical practitioners such solutions as telemedicine.

Welfare may seem a more contentious field impacted by IoT, yet it is worth considering the impact on such areas as healthcare, work, and communications. IoT enables many of the business processes which allow the healthcare industry address the growing challenges within their sector; at work, particularly manual labor and repetitive work, machines are becoming increasingly more intelligent and can assist humans with their tasks; and finally, the benefits from ever-improving communications, started with the early warning systems and more so with the content of the communications potentially providing detailed early warnings of natural disasters or emergencies, safety zones, and where rescue services may be located. But as explored, the story isn't all positive.

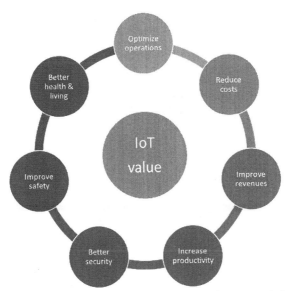

FIGURE 14.1: IoT Circle of Opportunities [Source: Machina Research, 2016]

Value versus costs

The positive outcomes of IoT are manifold and varied, and have been discussed earlier. There are, however, some less positive effects of IoT, which will require enterprises and individuals to approach the transformations with some preparation.

As shared in Chapter 10, the changes in culture within the enterprise will need to change. Not everyone will be ready or be willing to change, and to achieve the benefits and particularly the combinatorial opportunities behind IoT, commitment and support for the new ways will need to be in the enterprise.

There is a real concern that IoT will impact employment, particularly those performing fairly repetitive and manual tasks, which will be replaced by automation and intelligent machines. As we have seen, the progress of IoT has been fairly rapid, yet industries are far from replacing skilled workforces with machines. In many studies, enterprises are, in fact, seeing the greatest results where humans interact with machines to produce the best results. There remains, however, the threat to lower-skilled workforces on which many economies are fundamentally built. In these economies, policymakers will need to explore new ways to potentially incentivize enterprises with employees as compared to those benefitting from fully-automated systems.

Combinatorial innovation unleashed

In this chapter, the value of combinatorial opportunities has been discussed more than the actual opportunities themselves and what they may look like. It is important for chief innovation officers and heads of business strategy to first of all understand and pursue the financial benefits and opportunities from the initial implementations of IoT, but the important point is that once started, the opportunities from IoT are endless.

Compared to traditional IT and M2M projects, which were defined and planned in detail and outcomes precisely quoted, IoT starts its journey in this way by establishing a scalable, flexible, and agile infrastructure and architecture which ultimately grows and develops with the needs of the enterprise. This is where the combinatorial opportunities begin to emerge. Let's explore two or three examples to show how this may take place.

Transport industry: fleet management

Fleet management, defined as "...a function which allows companies which rely on transportation in business to remove or minimize the risks associated with vehicle investment, improving efficiency, productivity, and reducing their overall transportation and staff costs, providing 100 percent compliance with government legislation (duty of care)." Fleet management has made use of such solutions as telematics, and more recently, enterprises in this space have implemented substantially richer IoT applications such as track and trace, navigation, compliance, and security. For enterprises in the transport industry, the location of goods, transport, and staff are key information points. Here, direct and tangible benefits are clear, but this also begins the combinatorial opportunities for the transport enterprise with IoT.

Utilizing the same data, transport enterprises are negotiating improved insurance schedules, having removed greater risk elements in the process, and addressing many of the previously unknowns for insurers in their actuarial analysis. Knowing as well, the driving conditions, and times and behaviors of their drivers, transport enterprises are able to remote manage and recommend breaks, routes, and any immediate risks to the goods during the journey.

In these fleet management examples, combinatorial opportunities are mainly centered around internal data but extend this world, and consider the opportunities that are already present, where, for example, the largest fleet management companies are already sharing data from each of their vehicles about traffic and weather conditions, and through third-party traffic information aggregators such as INRIX, contribute to the overall improvement information about traffic around the world.

This is where the combinatorial opportunities for a transport enterprise may begin and continue to develop.

Lighting industry: lighting as a service

Traditional light bulb manufacturers such as GE, Osram, and Philips are transforming their industries from incandescent and fluorescent bulbs to LED bulb production with the added opportunity of changing the lighting fixtures to remotely manage the bulb and monitor its status and condition, enabling improved planning around maintenance and bulb replacement scheduling. This is, however, only the beginning. Once enterprises started to explore opportunities in lighting fixtures and from the potential data from these edge devices, it wasn't long before the list of sensors in lighting fixtures began to include motion detectors, infrared movement sensors, temperature sensors, and sound detectors to name some examples. Future examples may even include gas and other sensors.

For light bulb manufacturers, this has meant both fundamental changes to their manufacturing and business processes, their product development and management approaches, and their relationships with customers. It's unlocked a host of opportunities for lighting enterprises, and even today, customers are procuring lighting as a service rather than 100 bulbs.

Utility industry: a new approach in electricity

The traditional utility industry has been one of demand, subject to generation. What fossil-fueled solutions and atomic energy could provide became a limiting growth factor. Over-supply meant waste, and under-supply meant potential brown and blackouts. Supply was one directional, and optimization was achieved through the intelligent balance of loads across the grid.

This electricity industry is undergoing substantial changes. Distributed energy resources such as solar panels, wind turbines, and CHPs are contributing to overall energy networks. Attached energy consuming units are becoming more intelligent, enabling remote control and what has been termed, "demand-response" management. Energy storage solutions are improving, and electric vehicles and their charging stations are here. Finally, with a growing surplus supply of energy, energy trading in liberalized markets has also started to take place. For most of these developments, it is the common and unifying component of IoT or in industry parlance, "virtual power plants," that drives these changes. It's clear that what started as a way to help improve the usage by home consumers of their electricity through smart meters, and assist utility companies better manage their distribution and transmission grids with smart grids, has exploded into a substantially larger and richer ecosystem of opportunities for an ever-expanding group of stakeholders.

In the three examples, fleet management, lighting, and utilities, the immediate and direct value of the IoT solution unlocked substantial and associated values through a series of developments of which we have only seen the beginning. The share of the data with the *first receiver* solution in place has yet to become commonplace, and yet, it is now that chief innovation officers and heads of business strategy need to prepare for these changes.

The call for action on chief innovation officers and heads of business strategy

The examples above illustrate how IoT continues to be a disruptive market force. Connected devices, products, and services, and enhanced capabilities in IoT data and analytics are transforming industries. Enterprises need to prepare and ultimately participate in these transformations to remain competitive, and chief innovation officers and heads of business strategy need to assist boards and management teams understand the opportunities and value of the IoT. The *first receiver* can and should play a key role beginning with architectural considerations for the IoT deployment. It must also extend to training, to contractual relationships with product partners, supply chain partners, and others.

Identifying and prioritizing the right IoT applications, which delivers direct and associated savings and values to the enterprise, have become the new priorities for chief innovation officers and heads of business strategy in the enterprise. For some, they will be prepared; for others, they are preparing themselves and beginning to explore the challenges and issues in IoT. It is for this latter group that this book has been written, and shares the importance of the *first receiver* approach as a learning lesson from many of the earlier implementations and trials in IoT. It is a virtual certainy that IoT will change the landscape for almost every organization in some capacity. For many, that will mean advances tomorrow based on combining and adapting the advances from today. The rate of change will continue to increase, as will the opportunity. The *first receiver* architecture will provide the greatest opportunity for leveraging these advances to the fullest. The call to action for chief innovation officers and heads of business strategy is the same as for others in the enterprise: build and deploy the right architectures for IoT from the beginning.

Chapter 15

Seizing the Wave after It's the Wave: Investing in IoT Today and Tomorrow

With every wave, big or small, there is opportunity. This means opportunity for CEOs charting their organization's future and also for investors. Some will prosper; others will drown. There are very few sure things, but with a market as important and as massive as IoT, investors and non-investors alike should, at least, contemplate the opportunity.

Making the case for the *first receiver* becomes fairly straightforward if one believes in a few basic concepts. First, the baseline thesis is that IoT is here for real, and isn't a fad. The corresponding thesis is that the key value in IoT fundamentally rests on leveraging the utility value of IoT data (and insight and actions derived). One can augment that view with the recognition that there are already multiple vertical markets and specific use cases evolving from either M2M predecessor systems or early (albeit pedestrian) IoT implementations to more sophisticated, valuable, and effective IoT systems (as we highlighted in previous chapters). With that in mind, it stands to reason that the world in front of us has a number of areas where companies, governmental organizations, individuals, and investors can capitalize on the opportunity that has been created. This isn't unlike watching the Internet unfold in 1995, although one would hope that the lessons learned, good and bad, could be applied to how we embrace IoT moving forward.

Companies are likely to view their overall business more and more in the context of how their IoT-enabled company (amid an IoT-enabled world) can benefit. This means examining and reexamining every aspect of the company. Some will lose sight of their core competencies and go too far. Others will discount the impact of IoT and get left behind. To not thoughtfully consider how IoT will impact any company, or the opportunity that might be created for any company, would be management malpractice (and negligence on the part of boards of directors).

Government operations, most notably cities, must incorporate IoT. This will ultimately make service delivery better, cheaper, and create a quality of life that's central to the charter of some governments. This will happen faster in some areas than others, and of course, better in some areas than others, but over time it will become the norm, and hopefully the global adaptation will create new opportunities for all.

Indeed, everyone should take the time to understand how their lives can be made better with IoT.

M&A and the disrupting of the market

IoT is here. Nobody doubts this. We have already seen the signs of a significant market impact. The past three years were big for IoT M&A, as the major players in the tech stack and other key players engaged in the land grab. The bigger tech stack vendors (IBM, Microsoft, Oracle, Google, Amazon, HP, etc.) have a lot to gain and a lot to lose by not mobilizing, which in many cases means acquisitions to bolster their place in the market. There has been a mix of IoT and (more often) non-IoT buying leading up to today. Cisco has had a reasonably low investment in pure play IoT companies (like Juniper) to date, but have done many acquisitions in cloud, collaboration, and upgrading their network infrastructure capabilities. It would be shocking if that did not pivot to more specific IoT firms. PTC, on the other hand, bought Thingworx and then doubled down with Axeda, clearly showing their intent around Industrial IoT, which seems logical. They continued from there with others.

With a few exceptions, IBM has been similar to Cisco in their past buying, but it wouldn't be surprising for them, moving forward, to ramp their IoT acquisitions faster. It's hard to imagine GE and Siemens not aggressively continuing the path they've begun. They have as much as said that. Also, not surprising would be Samsung extending beyond SmartThings, and moving to other "things."

In 2014, Dell began setting up an IoT Lab in the Bay Area, and teaming with Intel on the Open Interconnect Consortium (OIC), and Microsoft has numerous initiatives, more enterprise-focused, along with their "Lab of Things" project. As for HP and Dell/EMC, they both have strong and widespread infrastructure investments, yet both are evolving from massive corporate restructuring and refocusing. While both have traditionally been acquisitive, it remains to be seen if they will buy heavily into IoT companies.

Then there is Rackspace, Amazon, and, of course, Google. Rackspace could have a lot to gain by getting serious about IoT. Amazon is there, with a serious and formidable offering and the platform to be a potential winner when this all shakes out. Time will tell. Google is also a done deal. They are all in, and have already been on a considerable buying spree for several years, from the well-publicized Nest acquisition to the complimentary purchase of Big Ass Fans, to their second half 2013, slightly less prominent buying spree of several humanoid robotics companies. They have quite the portfolio, and don't appear to be slowing down.

Last, Hitachi is a company that's been in both the information technology space and the operational/industrial space for a very long time, and ideally suited to be a key player as well. While they were quiet amid the PR drumbeat of others like Cisco, IBM, and especially GE, they had their own "coming out" party of sorts in 2016 with the announcement of the creation of the Hitachi Insight Group and the launching of the Lumada platform. Lumada appears to be a thoughtful architecture, especially in the context of leveraging data.

There has clearly been a great deal of hype about what will come, and most every company has some position on IoT at this point. But again, players like IBM, GE, Hitachi, Bosch, Siemens, Amazon, Microsoft, PTC, and others have so much at stake to gain (or lose), and have focused accordingly.

To date, there have been no obvious winners. The offerings that correspond to the focus, like GE Predix or Hitachi Lumada, are still very new. But with production instances of IoT projects ramping at a swift rate, and with these underlying efforts beginning to solidify, we will begin to see who some of the big winners will—and won't—be.

Monetization and the role of advertising

There is a lot of money being made from the Internet. This comes from commerce via sites like Amazon and eBay. This comes from online services like Shutterfly and PayPal. But more than anything, it comes from advertising. Because of the ability to personalize advertising based on collected profiles, companies know they can sell products and services through targeted online campaigns, delivered through sites like Google, Facebook, Tencent, Alibaba, and others. It works. So one of the obvious considerations around IoT is advertising.

The news in 2015 about Google possibly pushing ads onto refrigerators, thermostats, and such was compelling. It was interesting to see how shocked some people were in their reaction. Yet, the answer should be obvious. There is no end. For people who think there will be an end to the reach of advertising, wake up.

This is akin to a frog in water thing. You know, you put a frog in boiling water and it jumps out, but put it in room temperature water and heat it up and the frog cooks. Why doesn't the frog jump out? It acclimates to the environment. This is what we've been doing since the inception of the Internet. Think about it. When Amazon first started letting you know "you bought *The Goal* by Eli Goldratt, so you might also be interested in *The Race*, also by Eli Goldratt," you may have found that to be interesting, or you may have found it to be disturbing. You probably began to understand, however, the power of data. Then you may have noticed that when you surfed the web, online ads started to reflect your interests. Coincidence? Hardly. Then, the damnedest thing: two minutes before you walked by the Gap at the mall, you got a text ad from them letting you know about Gap's denim sale. We have seen for years how technology with beginnings in military use often makes its way into the commercial markets. Perhaps the cutting edge of counter-terrorism has played a role in guiding your choice in jeans.

It's a sign, not from some heavenly influence, but from the Gap saying they understand technology and how to reach you based on the online profile they've been collecting on you, helped by the 1000 other online profiles of you, provided by their advertising suppliers, who also want to make sure you buy those jeans. This is our world.

Now as we enter the age of the Internet of Things, a very logical evolution includes advertising. It shouldn't surprise anyone. Food products advertising on your refrigerator. Warm vacation getaways on your thermostat in the middle of winter. "Don't turn your heat up, turn it down while you fly JetBlue to the islands." Perhaps your Fitbit, linked to your phone, will suggest you enroll in a 5k, join an online dating service for men over fifty, and perhaps throw in a little "Low T" advertising for good measure.

On one level, many people will find this disgusting and overly invasive, and by all rights, it is. But it is a reality because it makes money. As bad as it may seem, there will be people buying those food products, taking those vacations, and spending money to change their lifestyles, and this validates the advertising investment through these evolving venues.

It shouldn't be surprising that some of the same models we've seen work in the past leaking into the IoT as well. Maybe you'll be able to get the Nest+ (ad free) for a premium. Maybe you can get your refrigerator for free if you allow the ads. Who knows? What we do know is advertising is here to stay. This certainty increases the need to consider standards, security, privacy, and, certainly, governance. Governance is a particularly tricky one from an IoT standpoint, in that you we must truly understand who owns the information that drives ads before ads can be purchased and the money collected.

The Internet of Things is an awesome step in the evolution of technology. It may at times seem like a revolution, but it's more of a fast evolution, like going from chimp to Tom Brady in a week. The wearable devices that were so cool, but toy-like in nature a couple years ago will be combined and adapted into the "must-have", sophisticated device that contributes to a longer, healthier life.

When and where to retreat

Just because there is a market, doesn't mean everything conforms to that market—or that any given model makes sense for any given idea. If there is any lesson we should have learned from the Internet bubble, it's that.

The dotcom failures happened for a variety of reasons, ranging from people and companies acting on hype without consideration of substance in a market that wasn't ready for online purchasing (like Toys.com and Pets.com) to markets that didn't exist and people were not ready to adapt to new modalities (like Flooz.com and Beenz) to those companies with "me-too" offerings, where only one or two would survive, like Lycos or Alta-Vista. Both search engines would have loved to be Google, but weren't. There is a frightening similarity between the numerous Google and Yahoo competitors that became irrelevant, and the preponderance of IoT Platform companies, who all seem to believe they represent the "leading" platform to IoT-enable the world. Spoiler alert: they probably do not.

Then there is the peril of moniker adaptation, meaning, XYZ becomes "XYZ.com" or "eXYZ." This became a bit of a joke in the rearview mirror for investors. The peril exists today.

Think about how loosely the term "smart" is thrown around. Smart systems, smart energy, smart grids, smart health, smart homes, smart cars, and more are all a part of the IoT umbrella, and companies that have XYZ products have increasingly offered "Smart XYZ products." But adding connectivity and renaming a product is no substitute for getting the fundamentals right, ranging from understanding the market opportunity to employing a thoughtful, workable delivery architecture. Many new IoT companies now mark the IoT world, each convinced they will capitalize on the burgeoning market.

Some will, but many won't, and for the very same reasons some of the Internet bubble companies failed. These were companies that had a decent read on the opportunity of the Internet, but failed nonetheless. Monitor110 had the arguably good idea to bring together relevant information for institutional investors via an Internet-based service. Yet, they burned though their $20M in funding and ultimately failed to deliver.[51] One of the founders offered his reasons for why the company failed in a published postmortem:

1. The lack of a single, "the buck stops here" leader until too late in the game
2. No separation between the technology organization and the product organization
3. Too much PR, too early
4. Too much money
5. Not close enough to the customer
6. Slow to adapt to market reality
7. Disagreement on strategy both within the company and with the board

---

51 http://www.businesspundit.com/25-internet-startups-that-bombed-miserably/3/.

Most savvy investors have this level of analysis in their DNA. It doesn't mean they always get it right, but the analysis of the basic principles highlighted above is something most do well, and will continue to do well, notwithstanding the hype of the market. Even so, IoT will cause many non-professional investors to place bets where this level of basic analysis won't be done. This is a mistake. And too, many companies engage business with "promising" IoT companies that will ultimately fail for the same reasons.

This is vaguer in nature, as some of these "failed" solutions will end up in the hands of larger consolidations that will bring them forward. Investing in IoT can mean anything from the actual funding of companies to investing money in the acquisition of products and services from these companies. And while there is potential failure across the entire IoT spectrum for reasons cited above, there are some obvious areas to steer clear based on market dynamics. Here are a few.

Platforms

There will not be thirty or 300 or 750 platform providers "winning" the platform wars. In the mid- to late-nineties there were many search engines that were all going to be the next, better version of Yahoo or Google. But the market won't sustain more than a few winners. Many of these companies will die. Larger players will absorb others, showing promise in some form or fashion, with sustainability. A few will succeed outright and on their own, but these will be the minority.

There are a few problems with platform providers. First, most got into the market aimed at IoT enabling products, so their customers have largely been product providers, not organizations (think: end-users). Therefore, many of the platforms in the market today cater to the implementation of closed-loop message-response systems. This is precisely the wrong direction for the market. This alone should scare most looking to either purchase these platforms or invest in their future. The possible exception are the ones that can architecturally adapt to meet the needs of organizations, primarily by implementing a *first receiver* capability into the platform architecture.

The second, albeit minor concern, is a function of any early success a given platform provider experiences with product companies that serves to re-enforce their belief that they have been successful in delivering what the market wants. In some ways, this is the innovator's dilemma, where the market advances but a given company fails to see the change based on current success. Platform companies are prime targets to experience this issue. Adding to this is the issue that most platform companies are generally comprised of people who know hardware, communications, and rules or workflow (alerting and triggering), but are largely void of people who really have "Data DNA," and are therefore more susceptible to missing the opportunity to service the enterprise because they don't really understand the importance of the utility value of the data and weren't architected to deliver that capability.

Isolated offerings

We are now moving past smart connected products. People (and organizations) are expecting IoT-enabled products to be minimally delivered with the contemplation of coexistence with a product system, if not a broader system of systems. Any isolated product that doesn't interoperate is likely to have limited appeal. This described many of the early IoT offerings, but should be a red flag to investors and companies alike.

This is especially important for commercial and industrial-grade systems, but will apply to everything. The least likely area of concern would, ostensibly, be wearables, but even there we are seeing a drive for integration, in both the ability to link disparate wearables into collaborating applications, as well as the ability to link multiple health related applications together, like MayMyRun with AppleHealth or MyFitnessPal.

Hardware

There will be winners in hardware, and there will be a lot of hardware. In the grand scheme of things, this is an increasingly commoditized market, and the barriers to entry are extremely high. Winners will likely come from a select few companies that already exist, like Intel, ARM, Freescale, and a few more specialty companies like Fitbit or Preventice, but the specialty companies are generally making their money on value-added services anyway. Most all research firms agree that the margins and opportunity associated with hardware make this a tough bet. For people trying to capitalize on IoT, this is unlikely to be the place to look.

Communications

The same discussion about hardware generally applies to communications. This is being somewhat commoditized at this stage. Not unlike hardware, there will be winners here for sure, but the margins are low and the barriers to entry high. The winners are already out there, mainly beating each other up to remain relevant.

The safer bets: trends and what appear to be the obvious opportunities

Even with the safer bets, there is certainly no guarantee of success. Just because a given market is big or hot, doesn't mean participation alone creates value. From a CEO or investor point of view, they are something to consider, and by in large, safer bets. While the list below is hardly exhaustive, it is worth looking at a few.

Security

As explored earlier in this book, well before IoT, security was a huge market. Whether you were in the security business, like McAfee or Sophos, or running a company like Ford or Target or a city like Chicago, the importance of security is unmistakable. The Internet of Things raises this to a new level. There have been many highly-publicized IoT-based hacks pointing to the vulnerabilities of IoT—and the massive exposure of such hacking on an individual and especially an organizational level.

In October of 2016, a massive attack was launched on Dyn, a New Hampshire-based company that monitors and routes Internet traffic. This resulted in users on the East Coast from accessing Twitter, Spotify, Netflix, Amazon, Tumblr, Reddit, PayPal and other sites.[52] The source of the attack was malware from phishing related attacks that get inside of networks and reach out to all devices on the network, then use those devices to spawn DDOS attacks of targeted sites. In this case, most of the participating devices were IoT-enabled products lacking the proper level of authentication.

The reach of IoT and the massively increased number of attack points coupled with the criticality of the exposed assets (traffic grids, power generation, large industrial operations, critical health devices) suggest that it is tough, if not irresponsible to underestimate the importance of security.

Service delivery: architecture

Over the short run, this architecture may be the biggest opportunity and underpins everything in this book. It points to leveraging the value in IoT, and not to any individual component technology or sensor innovation. As organizations install multiple IoT systems, they will increasingly appreciate the value of the data coming from the IoT subsystems. As this happens, enterprises will begin to demand ownership and/or control of the data from these systems. Using *first receiver* architecture where the creation of the IoT data is abstracted from the consumption of the IoT data, enterprises will be in a better position to leverage their data to the fullest while still providing the appropriate subsets of data to IoT product providers, remote corporate constituents, third party partners, and others as appropriate, like regulatory oversight bodies.

---

52 http://www.usatoday.com/story/tech/2016/10/21/cyber-attack-take s-down-east-coast-netflix-spotify-twitter/92507806/.

The market will value organizations (and solutions) that cater to this need. In many instances, organizations may lack the talent or wherewithal to effectively create or (more likely) adapt their technology architecture for IoT, and those organizations that can provide these very critical capabilities will be in high demand.

Service delivery: people

There is a gap in talent for IoT. Some people know technology, some know operational systems, but knowing both is a challenge, especially for executing an IoT strategy. The idea of the chief IoT officer is coming to light, as IoT implementations clearly cross boundaries between organizational leaders in technology and leaders in operational areas. Who owns the beacon system implementation at the retail store chain? The head of retail operations? The CIO? With IoT, organizations are recognizing that the lines are blurred. This will need to be reconciled, and there is a big opportunity for service delivery companies, ranging from staff augmentation via systems integrators to talent acquisition and especially executive talent acquisition.

Analytics, especially machine learning

On a broad level, "Big Data Analytics" is, in and of itself, a huge market. This has been gaining momentum for some time, and companies that perform these services are in demand, as are the growing number of tools on the market to make Big Data analytics easier, like Tableau, Pentaho (now a part of Hitachi), Datameer, and others. If Big Data analytics is big, then analytics associated with IoT will be equally big, if not bigger. This is in part because IoT is expected to generate so much data that the associated toolsets will be required in order to leverage the data. A basic analytics stack should include tools for monitoring IoT environments. This can mean basic BI tools like MicroStrategy, Information Builders, or BI tools from SAP, Oracle, IBM, etc., where used, can create dashboard fed by IoT data to quickly understand the state and direction of a given environment.

The analytic tools should also provide for exploratory analytics, where users need to navigate through the data, either looking for cause and effect, or establishing decision-trees and engaging in knowledge discovery for machine learning.

Then there are the predictive analytics. The market has embraced this fully, and predictive analytics associated with IoT-enabled products are expected. One does not need to be a genius to figure out that GE is suggesting they can deliver this with their platform named "Predix." It is a central theme in IoT, and an important one associated with the ROI expected with many IoT-related projects.

And while some have said predictive maintenance was the Holy Grail of IoT, others would argue it was simply the most obvious benefit of the data gathered from assets in a production environment. IoT is much farther reaching, and as the inter-relationships become more prevalent, the underlying digital signature becomes richer and richer. When that happens, machine learning can allow the migration from prescriptive systems to truly adaptive systems. When you consider the expanding reach of IoT, especially into the world of systems of systems, the notion of a world filled with systems that adapt to changing circumstances ranging from traffic flow to health conditions to production schedules all point to machine learning.

Smart home

One could make an argument that it is too late to invest in smart homes, and that this ship has sailed. But from the perspective of both investors and operators, there are two significant considerations. First, while the "winners" may be all but established, any of the key players in the market are winners because they consolidate and manage, but they all exist as umbrellas over a larger ecosystem where many can exist. So the considerations for market participants have as much to do with their ability to operate with Apple Homekit or Google Home or Amazon Echo, as their ability to deliver breakthrough functionality (or air-tight security, for that matter). So while the hub/platform winners may be established, there will still be many winning participants.

Secondly, this is a huge market. It isn't in its infancy, but the overall penetration rate is still very low, but the market potential is extremely large. This means a lot of money will be made here, and it demands attention.

Connected cars

This is a market going nowhere but up. It is focused on, but not limited to cars. This will extend to connected trucks, motorcycles, and other forms of transportation. The technology is advancing on so many levels, ranging from telematics to entertainment and information systems to advances in batteries where cars may get 300 miles on a fifteen-minute charge.

These systems are already evolving to consider more about our health and supporting our circadian rhythm, so, for instance, smart lighting can be utilized in ways that support natural melatonin production. Also, rather than turning on your fans to circulate the air, your CO_2 sensors will trigger the fans. The health of the home becomes a key part of this, so things like mold and bacteria growth are systematically addressed. The system will know the air quality in your home and interact with the HVAC system. Your home will become a homeostatic organism.

— Chad Curry
Managing Director at National Association of REALTORS

This isn't only the domain of every large auto manufacturer, but an entire cottage industry of technology providers that make up a much larger ecosystem that is expanding by the day. Not unlike security or other markets that are safe bets, there will certainly be winners and losers, but the market itself seems to be in a high growth phase for years to come.

Industrial IoT

In the article "Manufacturers Struggle to Turn Data into Insight," John Sobel, CEO of Sight Machine, makes a good point about the huge cost of getting things wrong in manufacturing, and the fact that many other industries have far more aggressive investments in analytics than the $11 trillion manufacturing sector. For the Industrial Internet of Things, everyone—from GE to Siemens to Cisco, PTC, Bosch and others—is investing huge resources. There remains much to do, especially in the context of the data.

This may be because of the legacy. John rightly points out that automation on factory floors has been around many, many years. Most of these systems are closed-loop silos, where the lifespan of data is fundamentally limited, and the exposure to that data is limited as well. The promise of the Industrial Internet of Things is rooted not only in the increased reach and sophistication of sensor technology gathering this information, but in the architectural migration from closed-loop proprietary systems to more ubiquitous access to this information both within and beyond the four walls of the manufacturing plant, or for that matter, the company itself.

The key to all of this is data. As older M2M systems become IoT-enabled, but from the lens of the operator or investor, the key might be the significant ROI associated with Industrial IoT. The regulatory issues do not exist, and the ROI is generally strong. The market demands (and proof points) are there, but the penetration remains low against the overall opportunity. Arguably, there is quite a bit of competition, but the opportunity is still compelling.

Retail IoT

One last area to note here is retail. The opportunity is arguably going to exist more for the big box stores and related component technologies, but over time will reach more and more of the market. Retailers like Wal-Mart, Gap, Macy's and more, along with restaurants like McDonald's, Subway, and others will have the scale and sophistication to IoT-enable operations.

This will span from basic distribution and inventory operations to customer-facing capabilities, like the use of beacons, facial recognition technologies, heat mapping, conductive ink-covered shelves and more.

At the heart of Retail IoT is the level of integration and insight. The goal will be to spend less and sell more at higher prices while creating a better experience for customers. This may mean understanding the optimal placement of goods based on adapting to flow patterns observed in a store, it may mean better managing and positioning inventory while reducing theft using conductive ink to understand exact placement and turn of products like razor blades at a drugstore. It may alert a restaurant to proactively redeploy equipment and change menus based on nearby events or conditions. If you're an operator, it will pay to understand these technologies, as well as the implications of the data being collected and how that can be used to better optimize your operation. If you are a technology company, it will pay to better understand how your products can play on this evolving world. If you are an investor, you may have a good opportunity to leverage these changes in the market.

Higher risk, higher rewards—not as obvious opportunities and bigger barriers to entry

There are other opportunities that will have enormous potential, but may be trickier based on regulatory issues and market entry issues. These will clearly attract investments and be the source of changed operating models and new strategies for leadership, but more complicated. There are also many emerging technologies that may represent fantastic steps forward in terms of capabilities, where the underlying technologies themselves are still somewhat new overall, or at least new in the context of IoT.

Healthcare
Healthcare IoT holds tremendous promise, but there are also substantial obstacles. Technology entrepreneurs must

understand and be prepared to navigate the regulatory maze, as well as the basic competitive and market considerations. Healthcare operators need to understand the opportunities, but also the regulatory, as well as operational and security issues that go along with new technology. Yet, sometimes the greater barrier to entry creates bigger opportunities.

As with other areas within IoT, with regard to healthcare, gathering data in greater depth across a broader range for a longer period of time, you can see patterns and gain insights that would otherwise be obscured. When you have a very thorough examination, your doctor won't only listen to you breathe and tap your knee to check your reflexes, she will have all kinds of blood work and other tests run, up to and including things like stress tests and EKGs.

In order to move the ball forward in digital health we need to see the entire elephant in the room and not a collection of isolated data. This includes qualitative assessments in PHM care plan apps, fitness tracker data, smart home products, medical IoT devices, electronic health records, visiting nurse notes, etc. At Senter we are working to reboot the approach to gaining insight from this data, and that is going to require combining all this data and validating it with clinical evidence.

— Sean Lorenz
Founder and CEO, Sente

More data is better. But it's usually costly, intrusive, and seldom readily available to the average person. The key is to somehow make it easier and more cost effective to get that data. This is the "Big Data" idea.

Correlating lots of different data sometimes reveals emergent patterns. Understanding your blood pressure, over a longer period with greater granularity, may still reveal limited information. Combining that information with blood sugar levels, temperature, steps taken, food ingested, and even external information, like ambient temperature or pollen counts or other air quality metrics can be combined for richer, more effective digital signatures that paint a telling story, and perhaps a predictive story that can trigger action to prevent illness. IoT and mobile health has the potential to greatly enhance the diagnostic and associated preventative measures to enhance longevity and quality of life while reducing the cost of service delivery. This creates an opportunity worthy of operator and investor attention alike.

Smart cities

If there are barriers to IoT implementation in healthcare, there are certainly barriers for IoT in government. These barriers exist on numerous levels. First, consider that procuring products and services in a government arena normally requires a bidding process. This shouldn't be a problem, except the bidding processes can be so onerous and resource-consuming that it may effectively exclude the small innovative startups.

There have certainly been efforts to open up accessibility, but those efforts are generally engaged by people already in government, who may not appreciate the implications of being a startup or small venture-funded company. In other words, they may think they have opened up a process, but in practical terms, they did not.

Secondly, there may be labor implications. For instance, in the State of Illinois, 94 percent of the IT staff are union members, who can vote to block any given RFP. This can be appealed based on need, then adjudicated via a process to address these situations, but the unions can effectively slow or stop initiatives that might otherwise be leveraging IoT for the good of the organization.

Lastly, the same union issues may come into play based on talent availability. Staying with the State of Illinois, a union member can apply for an open position of higher pay and stature, where qualifications may not be tightly written, resulting in people in jobs they may not be suited for given the changing landscape. Think of an orthopedic surgeon applying to fill the open position in neurosurgery. That person may be nice, and even a fine orthopedic surgeon, but you probably don't want him as your choice for your brain surgery, any more than you want the network administrator making decisions about how to index the database.

Aside from the obstacles above, government initiatives also generally take a lot of time and money. It isn't for the faint of heart. Yet, many companies had excelled at this. Accenture, AT&T, Cisco, IBM, and many others have strong business in government, and are staffed accordingly.

Some smaller firms make their way into government through larger companies, where they become sub-contractors underneath prime bidders. There is certainly a lot of money to be spent for smart cities and other government-based IoT initiatives, and there will surely be winners, but the hurdles may be a little more difficult.

Autonomous Driving

There has been ample discussion over the past few years about autonomous driving. This appears to be an extremely hot topic with far-reaching implications. Companies ranging from Uber and Lyft to BMW and others have a vested interest in this market. The technology is largely there today.

We have all heard about the Google car logging massive amounts of miles going up and down HWY 101 in the Bay Area. Pilots now abound. Nutonomy initiated self-driving taxis on a limited basis in Singapore in 2016 and expects to have them commercially available there by 2018, and operational with self-driving fleets in ten cities by 2020.[53] Ford is planning to make autonomous vehicles available to fleets in 2021, with sales to individual consumers to follow later.[54] At their annual shareholder meeting, BMW CEO Harald Krueger said that BMW

53 Yahoo News, 2016-08-29.
54 Reuters, 2016-08-16.

will launch a self-driving electric vehicle, the BMW iNext, in 2021.[55] Virtually all automakers, as well as most companies in and around the auto industry, are engaging in the race for driverless cars.

Yet, the reality of the prototypes and initial offerings are still expected to be well in advance of mainstream market acceptance, so if some industry experts are to be believed, the victory dance may be delayed for a while. One of the more optimistic outlooks comes from US Secretary of Transportation Anthony Foxx, who stated at the 2015 Frankfurt Auto show that he expects driverless cars to be in use all over the world within the next ten years.[56] Dieter Zetsche, chairman of Daimler, also predicts that fully autonomous vehicles, which can drive without human intervention and might not even have a steering wheel, could be available on the market by 2025.[57] More recently, the Institute of Electrical and Electronics Engineers predicted that 75 percent of cars on the roads in the world will be autonomous by 2040.[58]

One thing does seem certain: the progression to driverless cars is undeniable. It is also clear that while the ultimate market ten to fifteen years from now will look dramatically different than the market today, for now, the amount of money actually spent on driverless cars will be a small fraction of where it will evolve in the future. This isn't to say that technology elements for driverless cars won't be in demand, but rather, they will likely be incorporated more and more into traditional cars that are increasingly "connected and automated." Is there some ambiguity in the market now? There is. Is there disagreement on market direction? There does not seem to be. This just suggests the road may be longer and if you are an investor, the associated bets will need to be made with that in mind. And if you are in the automotive business, you need to be well down the road now, or you are probably being left behind.

55 Elektrek, 2016-05-12.
56 Frankfurter Allgemeine Zeitung, 2015-09-19.
57 The Detroit News, 2014-01-13.
58 http://www.naic.org/cipr_topics/topic_self_driving_cars.htm.

IoT-related technologies

Aside from sensors that are more and more sophisticated, connected through cheaper and faster communications links and deployed in a manner that leverages the utility value of the underlying data, there are several emerging technologies either targets to be embedded within current architectures or a complementary extension of those architectures that are worth noting. This list isn't meant to be exhaustive, but rather illustrative of now some emerging technologies may be integrated into IoT.

Drones

Drones should be interesting to both investors and operators. They are definitely growing in popularity. All you need do is visit a Frye's Electronic store or Best Buy or Argos and you'll see them on display. This technology goes way beyond the amateur videographer. Go online and query drones and police, and you'll find that a huge number of public safety organizations have drones in use today, and there is a growing cottage industry of drone suppliers and service companies. As we go forward, the increased capabilities of sensors deployed on drones, and capabilities of the drones, as well, will combine to make drones an important consideration in several use cases.

Drones aren't just for military or government/public safety use. They are being used for a myriad of use cases. Agriculture, for example, already uses a variety of capabilities, some IoT-enabled, for precision farming including yield monitors, soil sample results, moisture and nutrient sensors, and weather feeds. In addition to these historical datasets, new technologies, like drones, can provide a view of the current condition of the in-field crop. Another example is the maintenance of high value assets that are traditionally difficult and costly to maintain, like offshore oilrigs. UK company Sky-Futures is using drones to take images of offshore rigs and leverage sophisticated image processing to save time and money, improve the quality of inspections, and increase the safety of the workers by reducing or eliminating rope access inspection requirements and associated support vessel requirements and reducing shutdown time ultimately saving 80 percent of the costs and generating better results.[59]

Drones' acceptance and sophistication is growing. Moreover, organizations and government entities are recognizing that drone data can be combined with other IoT and operational data to create more granular signatures and great insight. It is highly likely the use of drones will only increase moving forward.

Augmented reality and virtual reality

Increasingly rich digital signature will also become the basis for leveraging augmented reality and virtual reality. There are compelling systems for asset maintenance utilizing augmented reality in production today, and those will only continue to evolve. Virtual reality will be used for training and situational analysis for everything from first responders to industrial operators and others, where the signature informs the VR experience and historical data is created by a wealth of IoT systems.

Distributed ledgers (AKA "blockchain")

Most people equate blockchain with Bitcoin. Certainly, that has been the highest profile use of distributed registers to date. Now there is growing recognition that distributed registers can and should play a key role in the Internet of Things. We should see an increased spotlight on this as organizations place greater and greater emphasis on a secure and transparent Internet of Things. One very good example of this is the "Chain of Things." The Chain of Things is developing integrated blockchain and IoT hardware solutions to solve IoT's issues with identity, security, and interoperability. They are leveraging the nexus between blockchain and IoT to deploy environmental, humanitarian, security, fraud, and efficiency-related solutions.[60]

Because there are so many devices expected to be in use

59 http://www.sky-futures.com/case-studies/saving-80-on-offshore-structural-inspections-2/.
60 http://www.chainofthings.com.

for the Internet of Things, both security and privacy are major issues. Distributed Ledgers will enable IoT ecosystems to break from the traditional broker-based networking paradigm, where devices rely on a central cloud server to identify and authenticate individual devices.[61] The costs to secure networks as vast as IoT will become prohibitive. Also, centralized servers can become bottlenecks, and are vulnerable to DDOS attacks. Distributed ledgers can enable the creation of secure mesh networks, where IoT devices will interconnect in a reliable way while avoiding threats such as device spoofing and impersonation.

While hardly a sure thing, and thus perhaps a riskier bet than certain elements of IoT, the promise of blockchain/distributed ledgers is already drawing quite a bit of attention, and could well be a key enabling technology for IoT in the long run. For operators and investors, this is a technology that minimally should be understood.

The call to action for CEO's and investors

IoT is an opportunity for executives and investors. One might suggest that gaining a strong understating of IoT is, in fact, and imperative for both executives and investors, as failing to do so will be to miss opportunities that may be unparalleled in their careers.

The Internet was a sea-change for business and consumers alike, and IoT will have an even greater impact. Getting it right will mean everything. So the call to action for organizational leaders is to ensure you have an executive team who understands IoT and do so in the context of your business.

IoT is technological and operational in nature, so the challenges and decisions to be embraced cross both boundaries, and need to be engaged by a knowledgeable team. This isn't an easy task, but an important one nonetheless. You should also ensure

---

61 http://venturebeat.com/2016/11/20/how-blockchain-can-change-the-future-of-iot/.

everyone understands the charter for the organization, and employ IoT to meet those needs. As the organizational leader, it is critical to embrace creativity and be open to changes in operating models. And last, it is critical to understand the value of the data. In this regard, you want to leverage data in a way that maximizes your opportunity, which also means maximizing the opportunity of your business partnerships as well, be they product suppliers, supply chain partners, or even regulatory agencies. Leveraging data is all about architecture. You may not need to be the one who dictates the architecture, but you should have an appreciation for what it means to get that right, or the ramifications of what it means to get it wrong.

If you are an investor, you should appreciate the areas where IoT likely can, and will make a huge difference. This also entails an appreciation for the hurdles associated with certain industries. Moreover, it means understanding the direction of the market. Investments in IoT-enabled products that don't contemplate the market demands and likely direction will be short-lived and disappointing. Likewise, a lack of appreciation of the talent demands and changing landscape can result in investments in great technologies that may not ever see momentum for all the wrong reasons. The talent aspects of IoT are nuanced, but organizations must be able to effectively deploy solutions for those solutions to be successful.